The Robertsons
Clan Donnachaidh in Atholl

The
Robertsons

Clan Donnachaidh in Atholl

James Irvine Robertson

Librario

Published by

Librario Publishing Ltd.

ISBN No: 1-904440-63-0

Copies can be ordered from retail
or via the internet at:
www.librario.com

or from:

Brough House
Milton Brodie
Kinloss
Moray
IV36 2UA
Tel / Fax: 01343 850617

Printed in Times.

Cover design and layout by Steven James
www.chimeracreations.co.uk

Printed and bound by
4edge Ltd, Hockley. www.4edge.co.uk

Gilbert Robertson of Struan, 23rd Chief
of the Clan Donnachaidh.

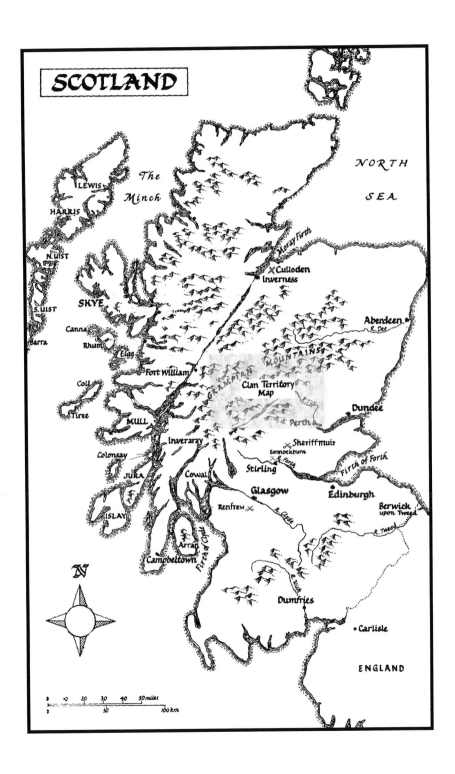

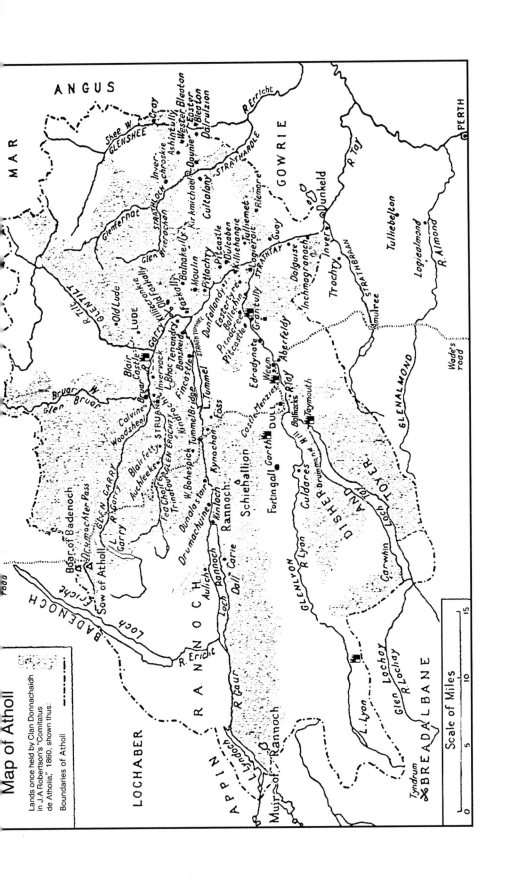

Map of Atholl

Lands once held by Clan Donnachaidh in J.A Robertson's "Comitatus de Atholia," 1860, shown thus:

Boundaries of Atholl

Scale of Miles

0   5   10   15

Contents

Chapter One

The Clan Donnachaidh -
'The Children of Duncan'

The landscape of Atholl can make the heart sing. Everything that makes the scenery of Scotland special is here - hills, lochs, heather, forests, castles, romantic ruins. On the high, empty moorlands the vast horizon is rimmed with mountains. In the intimate depths of the glens are tiny burns with tumbling waterfalls that eventually join the mighty river Tay.

Those whose roots are to be found here are blessed. They are not the offspring of barren deserts, urban squalor, or humdrum farmland. Instead their genes were cradled amid beauty and part of the most spectacular and romantic culture in Europe.

Clan Donnachaidh surnames are amongst the most numerous in Scotland, and each family will have its own story. But the Robertsons of Struan are the trunk of the tree. The descendants of Duncan, the first chief, married into the indigenous people of Atholl, commanded their loyalty and affection, and led them in both peace and war. So the history of the chiefs' line is largely that of the Clan as a whole. Descendants of Duncan became significant land holders in the north - Robertsons of Inches and Kindeace - and in southern Scotland - Robertsons of Ladykirk. But the vast majority of the Clan lived and died in Clan country - as likely did their forebears for thousands of years. They followed their chief; his history was theirs.

Situated just north of the Highland line, the great fault that splits the lowlands of Scotland from the mountains, the landscape of Clan Donnachaidh country was carved out during the ice ages. Glaciers from Rannoch moor sent out tongues of ice a thousand metres thick which rounded the tops of the hills and scoured out the straths and glens. The peak of Schiehallion, the great quartz mountain in the heart of Clan territory, stood clear of the frozen waste. At the edge of its summit of frost-shattered rock lies a huge granite boulder which once floated like a cork on the top of the ice and was marooned when the glacier receded some 13,000 years ago.

Modern travellers who enter the Highlands by crossing the river Tay near Dunkeld are moving through the most important of the rare passes that thrust north against the grain of the landscape. Like limbs from a tree, several straths branch west from the line now taken by the railway and the road.

The first after the river crossing is Strathtay which leads off at Logierait and meanders through what could easily be manufactured park land fifteen miles to Loch Tay, the sixth largest body of fresh water in the country. Carwhin at the west end of the loch was Clan land, as was a great tract at the east end. Dull, between the loch and Aberfeldy, is one of the most ancient settlements in Highland Perthshire and one of the earliest of Clan holdings. East from there, through the homeland of Clan Menzies, the north side of the river has a line of eleven estates whose boundaries have changed little for a thousand years. In their time most have been owned by Clan Donnachaidh lairds but only one - Pitcastle - today.

Schiehallion under snow from Loch Rannoch.

14

Travel on to Pitlochry, part of the old Clan estate of Faskally, which is the bustling tourist centre of Highland Perthshire. Over the pass to the east, itself a battleground which once rang with the 'sullen and hollow' clash of sword against sword, lies Strathardle which was dominated by the Reids of Straloch, offspring of a son of the Clan chief with reid or red hair. A mile or so north of Pitlochry the hills part again for Strathtummel and here was the ancient road to the isles through the heartland of the Clan. This is a harder landscape than Strathtay, just across the hills to the south, the soil less fertile and the moorland lower on the slopes. It leads past Loch Tummel with its drowned island on which was the first recorded stronghold of a Clan Donnachaidh chief.

Schiehallion commands here. Its huge bulk and isolation from neighbouring mountains gave it an importance in peoples' minds that is reflected in the legends and stories that accumulated to it. Its name means the Seat of the Caledonian Fairies. The road continues on towards the setting sun, past Dunalastair and the burial ground of the Clan chiefs, to Loch Rannoch. On its wild southern shore amid the Black Wood, a relic of the primeval Caledonian Forest that once covered Scotland, the 18th chief built a mansion in 1855. He was the last chief to live in Clan country on the land his forebears and his kindred fought and sometimes died to control.

The pass of Killiecrankie.

15

Back on the great road north, the river to the left is now the Garry which flows along the bottom of a great chasm at Killiecrankie, the scene of Perthshire's bloodiest battle. The pass opens out onto the Blair of Atholl, dominated by the wedding-cake castle of the Dukes of Atholl. The estate of Lude, once owned by the most ancient branch from the chiefs' line, marches with Atholl lands here and, as the road climbs out of the plain, it passes Invervack, the breeding ground of great Clan warriors, and Bruar the site of the Clan Centre and Museum.

Just before the high moorland closes in on the highway and it begins its run north to where the hill called the Sow of Atholl meets the Boar of Badenoch lies the very core of the Clan. Across the river at Calvine is set the tiny hamlet of Struan - *sruth*, a stream - the place from which the chiefs of the Clan Donnachaidh receive their sobriquet. Here is the Clan kirk where Clansfolk have worshipped and been buried for generations. The ancient artificial mound just upstream of the church is probably a mote hill where progenitors of the Clan gathered to see the administration of justice by their chief. This spot controlled the junction of the rivers Errochty and the Garry and protected the glen behind.

This is the mouth of Glen Errochty where the estates - Kindrochit, Auchleeks, Blairfettie, Trinafour - were all owned by Clan lairds and Struan himself had the rest. The narrow route through this glen climbs south, along a stretch of the first road to be built into the Highlands, to reveal the great whale shape of Schiehallion before it plunges down to join Strathtummel near Dunalastair or Mount Alexander where Alexander Robertson, known as the Poet Chief, built himself his Hermitage in the early 18th century. He called it paradise, a place set outside the world and its mundane concerns. In this, at least, his judgement seems sound.

Today the people living here speak English. The language used before that was Gaelic, prior to that Pictish. Place names such as Tay and Schiehallion derive from an Indo-European language even earlier - four changes in a couple of millennia. But humanity had been here for seven thousand years before that and we can only speculate on the cultural shifts in those vast time spans of prehistory. But the human stock probably remained much the same.

The progeny of those who first tilled this land and raised the stone circles or burial mounds that are still such a prominent feature in the landscape may have faced incoming warlords, chiefs and kings but these were absorbed by the people rather than replacing them. Only in the last couple of centuries did that continuity break as incomers replaced the indigenous inhabitants, many of whom have followed their predecessors overseas or to a better living in the Lowlands.

A break even more profound has taken place in the last half century. Until then the vast majority of the people here earned their living from the land. Now only a tiny minority are farmers. The understanding of the country and the seasons are no longer critical for survival. The hills have become a playground and only traces of the old Clan society can be seen in the landscape.

Chapter Two
The Beginning of History

History starts with the invention of writing and the first mention of the Highlands comes from the Roman historian Tacitus who wrote of the battle of Mons Graupius in 83 AD between the legions and the northern Celts of Caledonia whom he called Picts, or painted people. They probably wore tattoos or coloured their skins for battle. The Romans won the engagement but left the mountain tribes unconquered, instead retreating south behind chains of forts which became great defensive walls stretching scores of miles across the country.

Early records may be virtually non-existent but we can touch the minds of these ancient peoples through superstition and legends. Their world had another dimension, vestiges of which lasted right up to the 19th century. They could consult their ancestors who appeared in visions or in the tossing leaves of a wind-blown forest. Every task must be approached the right way with little rituals to appease the other world. The ceremony of Beltane on 1st May derives from worship of the Baal, a god of fertility who often demanded sacrifice. All Hallows' Eve was the night when the spirits of the dead were abroad. The belief in urisks, beings that inhabited water falls, could go back

A shian above Killiecrankie.

thousands of years, as do the water kelpies that disguised themselves as horses to snatch young girls and drown them. The Fury in Loch Glassie above Strathtay cannot go back much before the first millennium BC since she had teeth of iron - the most terrifying substance of its era - with snakes and eels for hair. All water housed supernatural beings, usually sinister.

The bronze-age burial mounds were shians, the homes of fairies, again creatures that were usually sinister and elaborate rituals must be performed to protect children from them. Otherwise a new-born baby could be snatched and replaced by a changeling who would sicken and die. How else could so many infants fail to survive? Cattle must have crosses made from wood from the rowan tree - mountain ash - bound in scarlet thread above their byres to safeguard them from spells that would dry their milk or make it sour through malign influences. Protection came from rituals and incantations, propitiating the sun and the spirits of ancestors. The sacred wells of druidism were taken over by the Christian missionaries but pilgrims still came to them for the healing water or visited the great stones which can cure most things including whooping cough (Kindrochit) measles (Fearnan), or breast ailments (Bolfracks).

The imperative of the seasons imposed a discipline that was unchanging. The harsh climate and poor soil required relentless toil to wrest a living from the land. Throughout the Highlands the ghosts of ancient field systems, the ruins of farmsteads and shieling huts go back for thousands of years. The tribal and clan groups that form in such circumstances were the norm in human affairs across the globe. In fact in 1816 Walter Scott wrote a 'Comparison between the

Kindrochit Stone.
Rainwater drunk from the cleft was the cure.

HIGHLAND CLANS and the AFGHAUN TRIBES'. He could have equally compared them to the Zulus or Masai in Africa, or the native peoples of America.

The classic clans grew in the early middle ages when kinship groups united to protect the land they depended on for survival against rivals. From the fifteenth century, the increasing power of central government and the rule of law combined with the overwhelming need to deal with the mighty southern neighbour led to rapid development in the Lowlands. But, isolated in their mountain fastness, the Highlands did not change and the two societies in Scotland became increasingly divergent.

The Highlands of Scotland held what has been described as the last tribal society in Europe, utterly different from the rest of Great Britain, its natives seen by outsiders as savage barbarians. North of the sharply defined border of the Highland line, people spoke Gaelic instead of English, wore tartan-patterned plaids - the plaid is a rectangular piece of woollen twilled cloth about five feet by sixteen which was folded so that it came to mid-thigh and secured with a belt. In the early 18th century, it was cut above the belt, the top half discarded and thus was formed the kilt - rather than trousers and carried weapons. Their music, culture, customs and many of their laws were different. In the far north-west, Catholicism had not only held out against the Reformation but itself battled against paganism. A mutual contempt was almost all the two societies had in common.

But this clan system contained the seeds of its own destruction. In the 18th century the Highlands held 30,000 trained fighting men who were an irresistible magnet for anyone fomenting trouble against the state. After the failure of Prince Charles's rebellion in 1746 when an army of Highlanders came to within 150 miles of London, the government deliberately and ruthlessly destroyed the culture.

Records hold little about the activities of the ordinary Highlanders whose progeny is now scattered across the globe. But their lives were bound up in those of their clans and chiefs. By understanding these their descendants can rediscover the history and way of life of their forebears.

Chapter Three

Origins of the Clan

The Scotti, a small tribe of Celts from northern Ireland, arrived on the western seaboard of the country around 500 AD. With them came the Celtic brand of Christianity introduced by St Patrick. St Columba, himself of royal Irish descent, crowned Aidan king of his new country of Dalriada in modern Argyll and, in 563, the saint and his kindred or clan were settled on the island of Iona where he founded a monastery and set out to evangelise the Picts who occupied the northern half of what is now Scotland. The next nine abbots were all blood relations of Columba for clerics of the Celtic church were not celibate but both married and fought in battle.

This period is the darkest of the Dark Ages and the following couple of centuries were a confusion of conflicts and shifting alliances, particularly in Dalriada which sometimes was reduced to being no more than a Pictish fiefdom. In spite of the turmoil the work of the monks continued. In 605, Adamnan became abbot of Iona and he sent missionaries into Atholl. At Dull in Strathtay, they founded a small monastic settlement which became the first college of learning in Scotland and spread the Gospel throughout Highland Perthshire. One of these evangelists, St Fillan, was the founder of the Clan kirk at Struan. Before being moved to Perth Museum his ancient iron bell was safe there for centuries. Any man who tried to steal it discovered that it became heavier with each

St Fillan's Bell

21

yard he carried it from the kirk until its weight rendered it immovable. This was the time when people built circular defensible homesteads - one was excavated in 2001 at Dunalastair and the ruins of others litter the hillsides - and great men topped most hills with fortresses such as Dun-mac-tuthail on Drummond Hill, Dunglass above Fortingall or Castle Dow ten miles down the Tay.

In 730 AD Angus McFergus, king of the Picts, ousted the Moraemar or petty king of Atholl and and took it over as a royal possession. It must have been one of the first Pictish kingdoms to be infiltrated by the Scots for the name itself derives from Flota, meaning New Ireland, first appearing in the Annals of Ulster in 739. A century later, in 848 the Scot Kenneth MacAlpine was able to claim the crown of both peoples, forming the nucleus of modern Scotland and he set up his capital at Dunkeld to which he moved the 200 year-old college of Dull.

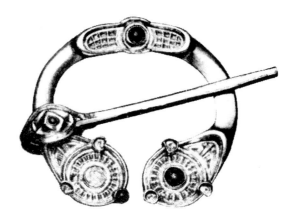

Dated as 9th century, this silver brooch was
found at the Pictish Palace, near Aldclune during
the building of the A9.

Malcolm II who died in 1034 was the last of the direct male line from Kenneth. His daughter married Crinan, lay abbot of Dunkeld and male heir to the Celtic earls of Atholl. Their son was king Duncan, famously murdered by Macbeth who was in turn killed by Malcolm Canmore. The latter's second son Malcolm fathered the 2nd Earl of

Atholl. The 3rd earl's eldest son predeceased his father and his granddaughters carried the earldom out of the old royal line but his second son was Conan whose name appears on charters soon after 1200 receiving grants of land in Glen Errochty. And he passed his Highland Perthshire lands to his descendants.

Far to the west, matters had deteriorated. The possessions of the Scots had been swamped by Vikings, the monasteries and abbeys sacked and raiding armies had penetrated the country as far east as Dunkeld, the last of these being defeated at Luncarty a few miles to the south in 990. The early records split the Vikings into three groups who struggled to dominate the western seaboard. The Fingall and the Dugall - the white or Norwegian Vikings and the black or Danish. The third category was the Gallgael, the Gaelic pirates. Although the latter intermarried with the northern Vikings they were, in essence, Picts and after centuries of almost continuous warfare and continuous dynastic intermarriages into kinship groupings such as the Kindred of Columba and the royal house of Argyll they overcame their rivals and, under Somerled, became Lords and Kings of the Isles.

Malcolm IV was King of Scots, a position little more elevated than Lord of the Isles, and he was both overlord of Somerled's mainland possessions in Argyll and his rival for power. In 1164 they met in battle at Renfrew. In Somerled's army were his allies from the Hebrides, Kintyre, Argyll and Atholl. The battle was lost and Somerled killed. Somerled's great-grandson Angus Mor, Lord of Islay, died in 1294. From his eldest son Angus Og descend the various branches of Clan Donald. From another son, Angus of Cowal, the earliest source, the Book of Clanranald, says 'from whom are descended the Clan Donchaid and Robertsons'.

Duncan de Atholia is considered the first chief of Clan Donnachaidh and confusion has attached itself to his ancestry. Up until the 19th century the Clan and everyone else knew that he was descended in the male line from the Lords of the Isles, progenitors of Clan Donald. This is stated in the oldest sources of both Clan Donald and Clan Donnachaidh. Then, in the 1830s, the Historiographer Royal for Scotland, William Skene, came to the conclusion that Duncan was descended in the male line from Conan, male descendant of the last Celtic Earl of Atholl, and not from Somerled, and so inherited his estates directly rather than through marriage. Skene had found a charter mentioning Andrew de Atholia as father of Duncan who was not mentioned in the traditional pedigrees and from this and the absence of reference to the Island kindred in Duncan's coat of arms, he decided that the accepted lineage was wrong.

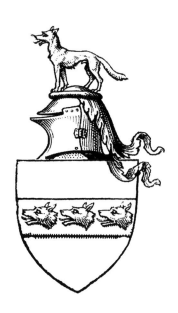

But Duncan the 14th chief, wrote on this subject a good sixty years before Skene and he pointed out that the old oral 'genealogies may be and actually are very much abridged.' He did not know of Andrew de Atholia but would have found nothing unusual about his omission from the traditional pedigree. The chief's coat of arms incorporates three wolf's heads. These are supposed to have been granted to Duncan because he rid Atholl of wolves, although the last Perthshire wolf is said to have been killed by a Mrs Robertson who bopped it on the head with a wooden potato masher when it entered her cottage to investigate the cooking pot

Arms of Duncan, the first chief.

over her fire. Mullinavadie - the Wolf's Mill - just north of Dunalastair in Strathtummel marks the spot. The potato did not come to Atholl until well into the eighteenth century which puts a rough date on this extinction or, at least, the story. However on an early seal St Columba is enthroned on a couple of wolves and the supporters of the chief's arms are a serpent and dove which again suggests descent from the Kindred of St Columba. And it has been speculated that wolves featured on the arms of the old earls of Atholl.

The kindred of the Columba also married into the Isles, so the wolf, the dove and serpent could have come through this route. Furthermore Alastair Campbell of Airds, the Unicorn Pursuivant of Arms, an expert on West Highland heraldry, states 'It is by no means unknown for an outsider to come in and, through marriage, to assume the effective leadership/ownership of a district. If an incomer was required to take over as local leader he would quite properly adopt arms pertaining or appropriate to his wife's family rather than to those of his own. There are plenty of examples.' He also points out that the earldom of Atholl was passed on through the female line after the death of Henry in c.1222. Conan of Glenerochie through whom Skene says Duncan descended in the male line is said to be the second son of Henry. If he was passed over for the earldom, then Alastair Campbell says 'at least there would have been grounds for a major row over the inheritance and the fact that there is no mention made of this would suggest that the issue did not arise - i.e. an argument for an Island descent in the male line, rather than one from Atholl.'

The inadequacy of the sources means that they are unlikely to provide definitive proof of Duncan's descent one way or the other. However the most plausible scenario seems to be that Andrew, son of Angus of Cowal, descendant of Somerled the Viking, married the great heiress of the Celtic royal line in Atholl. The Lords of the Isles were virtually peers of the Kings of Scotland at the time, so this would have been a marriage that brought added power, security and prestige to both families. As well as holding much of Atholl and Rannoch by royal charter their son Duncan was the blood heir to his mother and the charismatic leader of the indigenous people of Atholl. Thus was born the Clan Donnachaidh.

The Gaels believed that their chief held the land in trust for the ordinary clansfolk. In a hangover from the Celtic system, they also believed in tanistry - that they could select a new chief from the most suitable of the nearer male kin of his predecessor. The monarch's title was always King of Scots, but Malcolm Canmore and his successors busily turned themselves into kings of Scotland. William the Conqueror introduced the feudal system into England. He owned all the land. He parcelled it out to the knights who had come over from Normandy with him in 1066. They were the king's vassals, holding their estates which they could pass on to their eldest sons in exchange for operating the king's law and providing soldiers at his request. Similarly those great men could give or sell parts of their own lands in exchange for feudal services. So when the king wanted war, he told his nobles to muster their men and they in turn told their lesser barons to muster theirs and thus an army appeared. If anyone failed to arrive, then they were in rebellion and their lands would be lost.

Canmore's queen, Margaret, promoted Roman Catholicism in place of the Celtic church, and their son David I (1124-53), reared at the English court, brought north Flemish, Norman and Breton knights in his train, giving them land charters and vigorously pursuing the feudalisation of Scotland. So almost as soon as the clan system began to be formed it was in flux. Some clans held their land by the sword. Others by the consent and under the protection of some more powerful neighbour. Others had charters from the king. The latter was the hardest reality. It said the land was the chief's, not the clan's, and his eldest son would inherit, not the best of his kin. The monarch's charters were issued at court and covered the whole of the country. Granted his power might not stretch as far as his parchment but, without the precious document, a clan could be threatened by a covetous, well-armed and well-papered neighbour, for such a man could call for support from the forces of the law and the slowly accumulating power of the king.

Andrew de Atholia's lands were centred on Glen Errochty at one end of which lay Strowan or Struan from which his successors took their title. The spelling has varied down the ages. Only in the last century has 'Struan' become universal. The size of the estates of early chiefs waxed and waned. The turbulent history of Clan Donnachaidh has meant that charters and papers have often disappeared and land ownership changed hands frequently as the king sought to reward his followers, or when tracts were hived off by chiefs as marriage settlements to daughters. But the early Clan was a constant presence in the shifting land ownership in Atholl. Andrew and his two successors were described as 'de Atholia' - of Atholl - which was a firm indication that they had anciently held these lands.

Chapter Four
Duncan de Atholia

D uncan is said to have been born in the 1275, just in time to take part in the opening rounds of the War of Independence against the English. Traditionally William Wallace sought refuge in Atholl after his defeat at Falkirk in 1297 but one is on surer ground when when considering the chief's relationship with Robert Bruce. John Baliol was installed as Edward of England's puppet king in 1292 but his master removed him four years later for 'contumacy' leaving the country without a monarch. Bruce and the Red Comyn were rival claimants for the throne. At a meeting in the Franciscan priory at Dumfries in 1306, Bruce slew his opponent in front of the high altar. Alastair Macdougall, Lord of Lorne, was married to the dead man's aunt and therefore now had a blood-feud with Bruce.

In 1306 Bruce was crowned at Scone and soon after was routed at the battle of Methven. He, his queen, and a few followers escaped into Atholl and was received by Duncan. He had his stronghold in a castle on the island in Loch Tummel, which was submerged in 1950 when the loch was raised by five metres by a hydro-electric dam, and Bruce took refuge in the the Wood of Kynachan just a couple of miles to the west. A ford on the Tummel, now beneath Dunalastair Water, was the King's ford. The King's Hall was in the woods to the south and the Queen's Pool was a little further downstream. Strong tradition tells of an unrecorded battle between Lochs Tummel and Rannoch at this time. Innerhadden was where the battle started, Dalchosnie next door means field of fighting; Glen Sassunn is the glen of the southerners, the route taken by the enemy troops. The result was a victory thanks to the women of the Clan who supported their menfolk by filling stockings with stones and using them as clubs to devastating effect.

With Duncan and his Clan by his side the king ventured west and was defeated at Dalrigh (the field of the king) near Tyndrum by the Macdougalls of Lorne and retired back to Strathtummel. In this battle the king lost the brooch with which he pinned his cloak and this is still in the possession of the victor's descendants. Eight years later the Clan went down to Bannockburn to fight alongside Bruce to defeat the English and make him undisputed king of Scots.

Bannockburn, of course, is the seminal battle in the fight for Scots independence from England. As a result every clan wishes to claim that it was part of Bruce's army. The earliest written reference to the participation of the clans seems not come until 1822, when the historian David Stewart of Garth listed twenty one Highland chiefs that were there, but he gives no source for the information.

The Brooch of Lorne.

Snatched from King Robert Bruce at the Battle of Dalrigh 1306 when he and Clan Donnachaidh lost to the Lords of Lorne. It is in the possession of the Macdougalls of Dunollie.

As far as Clan Donnachaidh is concerned, there is a very strong logic that Duncan, unquestionably a close associate of the king, would have been there with the Clan and he is one of those on Stewart's list. As well as strong logic, there is strong tradition that supports this. Clan Donnachaidh is said to have been a little late for the conflict, and were part of the contingent that came down from Gillies Hill at the decisive moment of the battle and these reinforcements tipped the balance in Bruce's favour.

On the bare framework of this tradition an elaborate account of the Clan's involvement in the battle has been constructed which ends with the victorious king declaring 'Hitherto ye have been called the sons of Duncan, but henceforth ye shall be called my children.' This explanation of the origin of Robert-son as the Clan's primary surname actually predates its first use by well over a century.

The Clan had several more encounters with the Macdougalls. The only record of one was written down by Ewen Macdougall, Clerk to the Earl of Breadalbane at Taymouth, in the 1820s and describes the aftermath of a cattle raid or creach against Clan Donnachaidh. The Macdougalls were tracked west and the two forces met in Glen Orchy 'where they fought bitterly, the Rannoch men were slain and their Chief fled with difficulty. The slain were buried and the cairns are still called Cairn nan Rannoch, or Rannoch Men's Cairns, and their arms cast into a small Loch near the Cairns called Lochan nan Arn.' It seems likely that this is a traditional local interpretation of Bruce's defeat at Tyndrum after which the losers' weapons were also said to have been thrown into the loch. If so, it would indicate that the bulk of Bruce's army were Clan Donnachaidh men, and that the ordinary Macdougall warriors were more pleased to have defeated them than the king. The monarch must have been a remote figure to most people, intent on consolidating his national position. Duncan's followers were local rivals against whom clashes must have been frequent.

However with Duncan at its head the Clan was usually on the winning side. It is possible that his most famous meeting with the Macdougalls is an amalgam of several skirmishes, particularly since the date given by one source of 1338 would make him past his prime for legendary feats of agility. They sent an army into Atholl and Duncan, disguised as a beggar, entered the enemy camp to scout it out. His cover was penetrated and he had to flee for his life. He chopped down one of his pursuers and then jumped across the chasm of the river Errochty to escape. The spot is now beneath the dammed Loch Errochty so the distance, variously reported between 11 and 16 feet, cannot be confirmed. His Gaelic name Donnachd Reamhar (pronounced 'rav-ar') means literally Fat Duncan, but a gravitationally-challenged warrior in his mid-fifties is unlikely to have managed such a leap. 'Robust' or 'stout' would surely be a more accurate translation. Another of his sobriquets was Gaisgeach Mor Fea-Chorie - the great hero of Fea Corrie. The corrie, a remote cleft in the hills west of Trinafour, was the muster point for Duncan's warriors before any campaign. It, too, is submerged beneath Loch Errochty

The battle was the following day. At first light, the chief's standard was pulled from the ground and with it came the Clach na Bratach - the Stone of the Standard. This snooker ball-sized globe of rock crystal is one of several charm stones to have survived. That of the Stewarts of Ardvorlich is the Clach Dearig - the red stone. The Campbells of Glenlyon had one but theirs was given to them by a visiting 'wizard' in the 16th century, presumably part of his stock in trade. Such stones have been made and venerated in all cultures for millennia. They are to be occasionally found as grave goods in pagan Saxon burials and would have had religious or mystical significance in pre-Christian religion. But how one came to be in the wilds of Atholl can only be guessed at.

The Clach na Bratach is the most famous and has the oldest history of any of these stones. It was said to be carried into battle before the Clan confined in a little cage on top of the standard pole. Otherwise it lived in a silken purse, the last

The Clach na Bratach, on display in the Museum at Bruar.

knitted for it by the Countess of Breadalbane. Its prime function was for healing. Any water in which the stone had been dipped had curative properties for both man and beast. It could also predict the future. When the stone became cloudy, it signified the approaching death of a chief. The consternation of the Poet Chief in 1715 when he consulted the Clach before going off to fight in the Rising can be imagined when he saw that it had developed a great crack through its heart. Perhaps it told the truth. If Struan had not joined the rebellion, his own fortunes and that of his successors might have been very different.

With the newly-found charm, Duncan and his Clan trounced the Macdougalls and captured their chief. He was imprisoned on Eilean nain Faoileag - the Island of Gulls - now topped with a castellated Victorian tower, at the west end of Loch Rannoch. A man rowed out with a barrel of apples. These were upset and during the confusion as the guards scrabbled around to retrieve them, Macdougall took the boat and escaped, leaving his captors marooned. An older version of this story has Macdougall living in comparative freedom under parole and breaking it to make his escape.

Duncan's death and its circumstances appears in a manuscript written by Duncan the 14th Chief in the eighteenth century. He said he was copying what originally appeared in the Red Book of Clan Donnachaidh which was destroyed in a fire at Meggernie Castle, Glen Lyon, in the 1650s.

'Duncan desirous to have the whole or some part of his large possessions secured to him and his posterity by written rights from the crown repaired to court which was then at Scoon or at Perth. He had his enemies but it seems they could not prevail against his favour with the King; his business was finished of an evening, and next morning he was to pay his court and receive charters from the King's own hand. Besides other occasional attendants he always had twelve chosen servants about his person but one of them was a traitor, Blair by name who was bribed to destroy his master. This he actually accomplished for when Duncan was getting himself dressed in the morning for his appearance at Court, Blair with his fist struck a razor or knife into the crown of his head, and then attempted to escape, but his master drove a chair at him which broke his back and Kenneth McGilivie another of the servants dispatched the traitor with a spear. All this was hushed up for the time. Duncan immediately caused his head to be bound up with bandages and caps and went to Court. The King observing his countenance as well as the tying up of his head,

31

asked of him what was the matter and he answered that indeed the Gentlemen of the court had made him sit up and drink more than was fit for a man of his age. He received his papers and departed but had not gone far from court when his People were obliged to put him in a litter; his papers were laid under him, he ordered his men to carry him to Dull and not to slacken their speed whether he was dead or alive, and if he should die by the way his body was not to be touched till his son Robert should arrive. Robert found the charters and buried his father at Dull where his grave is shown to this day as a rarity for its length.'

Duncan married twice, once to a daughter of the Earl of Lennox through whom he secured Rannoch and secondly to the co-heiress of the Ewen, Thane of Glentilt, and thus greatly extended his lands. By his second marriage he had a son, Patrick who obtained Lude and his descendants held that property for the next five centuries.

But others were establishing a presence in the neighbourhood. The original Menzies was one of those Flemish knights who came to Scotland to make their fortunes. The family had land in Atholl before 1300 and, like so many others of their kind, they founded a clan. The Stewarts, from Brittany in France, also arrived in the area. Walter the Steward married Bruce's daughter and their son became king. He held the earldom of Atholl himself and granted it to his son in 1375. In his 'Book of Garth and Fortingall' 1888, Duncan Campbell, the schoolmaster in Fortingall, delightfully described the first Stewart Earl and the arrival of others of his kin thus: 'His revenue and estates were not very great, but he had a great many allies, and pretty numerous company of gentlemen of his own surname to surround his motehill and fight under his own banner. Some of these Stewarts were cadets of his own house; many were collaterals that had been called in from Lorne. A few were descended from the Walter of Atholl line, and more than a few from the Wolf of Badenoch. To these were added Stewarts who boasted ancient or illegitimate descent from kings and princes who, when hunting the deer, wooed Highland maids in sequestered glens.'

Time and time again over the ensuing generations members of Duncan's Clan would marry Stewarts. Time after time over the years their interests would coincide. In combining to defend all Atholl they would gain the reputation as the most formidable warriors in Scotland.

Chapter Five

The Angus Raid and
the Barony of Struan

Duncan's successor was his eldest son Robert de Atholia, said to have been so named in honour of his father's friend King Robert Bruce. This seems perfectly feasible since the name had not been previously used by the family. His first wife was due to inherit Glen Esk in Angus but it went instead to her sister's husband, Sir Alexander Lindsay. This rankled although the chief married again and obtained other lands near Perth. By now Alexander Stewart, the Earl of Buchan and son of the king, better known as the Wolf of Badenoch, controlled Garth Castle. This grim little tower dominated the pass between Strathtummel and Strathtay.

The fluidity of local land holding is shown by Garth. The Menzieses are the first recorded owners. Next it was owned by Duncan; his son returned it to the Menzies as tocher or dowry for his daughter. A Menzies daughter then married a bastard son of the Wolf and it went to the Stewarts. These changes took place between 1320-1380. It was finally sold by the Stewarts in 1834. Although such lands may have changed ownership the people who farmed them remained much the same. Duncan Campbell wrote in the mid-19th century: 'The Chief of the old Atholl clan afterwards called Robertsons and Fergus, son of Aod or Aoidh, were lessees of Fortingall and other thanages before (the Stewarts) appeared on the scene. I think the Macnaughtons and Robertsons are the people of longest descent in Fortingall'.

The Wolf ran his lands in the Highlands as a robber baron, gathering a band of fiercely loyal followers as disaffected as himself with the king. The Wolf had his charters but he never paid his feudal dues and held his land by the sword. It is an indication of the lawlessness of the times that the Clan Donnachaidh was his ally.

At least two of the Wolf's legion of bastards were based in Atholl, Duncan and James who married the Menzies daughter and obtained the charter of Garth. Their uncle was Regent of Scotland and an enemy of

Garth Castle controlled the pass between
Strathtummel and Strathtay.

their father so when the chance came in 1391 to make trouble, it was not missed. Sir David Lindsay, holder of the Glen Esk lands claimed by Robert, was the very flower of chivalry. He had recently bested Lord Welles at a joust on London Bridge in front of King Richard II and his court. He tried to organise a parley to discuss the lands disputed by Robert. The Clan chief failed to arrive at the meeting place and Sir David sent spies into Atholl to discover what was going on. They never returned.

Clan Donnachaidh - led by Thomas, Patrick, and Gibbon the younger sons of the chief - and the Stewarts decided that violence was more to their taste than talk. They mustered some 300 of their followers and launched a raid into the Angus glens, burning houses and stealing cattle. An initial attempt by the victims to recover their beasts was beaten off but it gave time for a larger retaliatory force to be organised. Under the Sheriff Sir Walter Ogilvy, the Angus men who included Sir David Lindsay and other mounted knights hotly pursued the Highlanders who were withdrawing with their plunder. The two forces met at the watershed between Moulin and Strathardle and a vicious running battle ensued. A mounted man in armour was the tank of the day and it should have been no contest, but the terrain was unsuitable for the great horses and the opposition was nimble. The Angus men were routed and many of their leaders killed. One Highlander was skewered to the ground by Sir David's lance, but he wriggled his body up the shaft and, before dying, delivered a blow to his assailant which penetrated the armour on his foot and cut it to the bone.

The Lindsays gathered their full strength and launched an invasion into Atholl to seek vengeance. They met the Athollmen once again on the boggy watershed and again the Angus force was defeated. The government issued an Act of Forfeiture naming Clan Donnachaidh, one of the first clans to appear in history, and the chief was deprived of his lands in north Rannoch. They became Menzies possessions but brought their owners little more than trouble over ensuing centuries. The natives were always lawless and outwith control.

Duncan, the third Chief, was sufficiently significant a figure in the nation to be one of the twenty nine noble hostages who went to London as hostages on the release of James I in 1432 and he likely died down south. His son Robert Riabhach - grizzled, pronounced 'riu-vuch' - is said to have bequeathed the surname Robertson to the Clan but in his time a surname was rarely necessary; both he and his younger brothers had been called the Duncansons when they were named by the authorities as participants in the Angus Raid.

Aside for one aberrant Campbell, the earldom of Atholl had ricocheted between the king and various members of his family since the time of Bruce. Earl Walter of Atholl had schemed for years for the throne. In 1437 only his nephew James I and his infant son stood in the way and a conspiracy was hatched by Walter, his grandson Robert who was the king's chamberlain and the disaffected Sir Robert Graham. The king had made himself vulnerable by trying to enforce his authority and curb the lawless nobility. In February James was assassinated in Perth but Walter had miscalculated and there was outrage, forcing the conspirators had to flee.

Sir Robert Graham and his outlawed followers found refuge the forest which then covered Glen Mor behind Schiehallion and they lived by plundering the surrounding countryside. Robert Riabhach joined forces with the Wolf's grandson John Gorm Stewart, - gorm means blue, the colour of plate armour. Together they destroyed the rebels and captured Sir Robert as he cowered beneath the shelter rock by Loch Bhac (pronounced 'Vac') between Blair and Strathtummel.

Robert is said to have been offered the earldom of Atholl by the new king but, perhaps thinking this a small honour compared with the antiquity of his name, he settled for a baron's charter (A baron administered justice on his estate) of his lands, which at that point covered a thousand square miles, calling them Strowan. He also received the addition to his arms of a crest showing a fist holding up the crown

The Shelter Stone by Graham's Burn, Loch Bhac, where the king's assassin was taken.

and the wild man in chains beneath the shield. The regal crown is a unique distinction in Scottish heraldry. Robert attended the king at Perth in 1451 to receive his reward. He lived another ten years before being fatally wounded in a skirmish with an old adversary, Forrester of Torwood whose uncle, the Bishop of Dunkeld, held lands which Robert considered his own.

Arms as used by the Chief in 1700.

Robert's successor Alexander was the first chief to call himself Robertson. Little is known about him although he continued the feud with the Bishop of Dunkeld. One of his Clansmen was arrested by the bishop for cattle theft and Alexander went to his rescue, attacking the cathedral whilst Bishop Lauder was saying Mass. The cleric had to take shelter in the rafters to escape a shower of arrows. This chief married twice, his first wife a descendant of Robert Bruce, his second a daughter of the Earl of Atholl and niece of James II. He had seven sons from whom many of the cadet branches of the Clan descend. These younger sons were each granted estates in Atholl and their younger sons and daughters would have found spouses amongst the folk on their land and thus brought a fresh injection of royal blood and the chief's line into their myriad of descendants.

Dunkeld Cathedral was made ruinous at the Reformation.

Chapter Six

Executions and Turmoil

R obert's eldest son, another Robert, died before his father and his
son, the 6th Chief William, was therefore the grandson of his
predecessor. He succeeded in 1508. The story of the family now takes
a sharp decline. The battle of Flodden against the English took place
in 1513. The king and many of the Scots aristocracy were killed. The
country faced a regency and the hold of central government which
had never been firm slackened still further.

The sources clash about William. What is beyond question is that
the Earl of Atholl managed to obtain a large chunk of his lands in
1515. A year later someone was beheaded at the hill behind Logierait
by order of John, Duke of Albany, who was regent during the minority
of James V. This site was originally an Iron Age hill fort and then a
hunting lodge of the early Stewart kings before becoming the place of
execution for Atholl until the mid 18th century. It stands above the
Tay and Tummel ferries and, before trees encroached, visible to a
great tract of the countryside and all travellers coming north, south or
west. William MacPatrick Robertson, a cousin of the chief, along with
his uncle were those decapitated say some historians. They state that
William the chief had a feud over boundaries with the Earl of Atholl
and met his end at the hand of the Earl's men in 1530. The Red Book
MS says that 'William burnt Blair castle and was afterwards surprised
and murdered by some people belonging to the Earl of Athol.'

But other authorities differ. The Chronicle of Fortingall was
written contemporarily by the Dean of Lismore and his son. In 1509
it had noted that 'John Cunnison of Edradour by Moulin was slain by
William Robertson of Strowan' and for 1516 it states 'Death of
William Strowane Robertsone who was beheaded at Tulymat on the
7th day of April'. Duncan Campbell says that the laird of Struan led
an army of his own followers and Rannoch Macgregors commanded
by the notorious Duncan Ladosach, which gave him 'a band of
upwards of 800 warlike and unscrupulous freebooters' which held
together for three years before William was caught by guile whilst

sojourning with his uncle John Crichton and executed. Campbell's authority comes from traditional tales and the historian George Buchanan who was tutor to James VI. The havoc in Atholl drew 'Buchanan's attention from the intrigues of courtiers and ecclesiastics'. He writes in Latin that MacRobertus Struanus was the man executed and he meant, without question, William, son of Robert, and the chief. One writer suggests that all three were executed - the chief, his cousin and his uncle,

Whichever way William lost his life, he also lost most of his estates. In 1515, the Earl of Atholl acquired a great tranche of Strathtummel including the island and the chief's stronghold there, most of Glen Errochty, the Kirktown of Struan and several outlying properties on the Tay. These lands were 'Apprised by a decreet of the Lords of Council from William Robertson of Struan, for default of payment of a debt of 1592 pounds Scots'. Estates throughout Atholl changed hands over the centuries but the family of Struan lost these for ever. One suspects that the debt may have been for damage caused by the 'band of freebooters' and the lawless William would not pay, even if he could.

In theory this change of ownership meant that the chief lost control of the greater portion of the Clan. However the practical implications of this loss of the chiefs' power was slight, for usually the interests of the Clan Donnachaidh fighters coincided with those of the Atholl family, the Stewarts and the smaller lairds. If they did not, then the Clan went its own way. In 1587, in a roll of Highland clans it states that the 'Clandonoquhy' was amongst those that have 'capitanes, cheiffis, and cheftanes quhome on they depend of tymes against the willies of their landlordis.'

Over the preceding centuries these lost lands had been farmed out to the sons of earlier chiefs and now the heirs to these men became feudal vassals of the earls of Atholl rather than their chief. The classic clan had all its land owned by the chief who gave leases or tacks of one of two generations to the senior cadet branches of his family. But these Clan Donnachaidh cadets received charters from the earls and held their land in perpetuity.

Other junior branches of the Clan in Atholl such as the Robertsons of Lude and Faskally obtained charters from the king and, again, the chief had no legal authority over them. Just as these men were vassals of the king rather than of Atholl or Struan, they had their own vassals, probably originating in younger sons of their own families, who gave their offspring and dependents tenancies on their estates. Faskally, for example, was the superior of the Robertsons of Calvine and Kindrochit who thus had to follow him in times of strife. In 1723 the Duke of Atholl, had 31 Stewart vassals and no less than 27 Robertsons and two Reids. Just before the Rising of 1745, it was estimated that there were 800 warriors of the Clan but 500 of these followed the Duke of Atholl rather than their chief.

The 7th Chief, Robert, was an infant when his father died and not until 1545 did he secure all the charters for his remaining lands, still called Struan, which were to remain of much the same extent for the next couple of centuries. These were the classic run along the south side of Glen Errochty and on into Rannoch. Later he received a charter for Disher, now Fearnan, on the north side of Loch Tay.

This Robert, who married a daughter of the Earl of Atholl, only briefly appears in history but the district was highly unsettled at this period and the fundamental reason was the rise of the Campbells of Glen Orchy who eventually became earls of Breadalbane. With their origins on Loch Awe, a succession of highly effective and ruthless lairds spread their power along the length of Glen Dochart and Loch Tay, coming to an abrupt halt at the edge of Atholl since its inhabitants were strong enough to rebuff their further attempts at expansion. These Campbells exploited the law in the shape of bonds and charters and backed it with executions and murder. One mysterious branch of the Clan Donnachaidh, the Robertsons of Carwhin on the north of Loch Tay, were displaced but the prime sufferers were the Macgregors. They lost Balloch, where the Campbells built Taymouth Castle, and eventually their entire territory. The only way that the clan could survive was through banditry. Many retired to the inaccessible wilderness north west of Loch Rannoch where Menzies held the charters but could exercise little control and from there they ventured out to plunder Atholl.

In the entry for 1531 the Chronicle of Fortingall reports that Rannoch, presumably the anarchic Menzies-owned north, was harried by John, Earl of Atholl and by 'Clan Donoquy' and that one of the

41

captured wrongdoers was 'heddyth' - beheaded - at Kinloch Rannoch. But it would take more than a bit of harrying to control the Macgregors. In 1545 the house of Trochry west of Dunkeld was burned down by them. They captured Robert Robertson of Strowan and killed four of his servants. The chronicler ends this entry with 'May the just God repay everyone according to his work'. It was probably after this incident that the chief built a stronghold at Invervack as his primary residence but this lasted little more than century.

Taymouth Castle.
Built in 1810 on what were
Macgregor lands in Atholl.

The Campbells may have had both the law and might on their side but the sympathies of many lay with their victims, even if they did so often seem to provoke their powerful enemies. Sir Colin Campbell, the Grey Laird, who now dominated Loch Tay, was fostered as a boy by the Macgregors but he was their most ruthless oppressor. It was said that he suckled hounds at the breasts of captured Macgregor women so that they would recognise the scent of that clan and track its members.

Colin Campbell, the Grey Laird.

One story tells of these Black Hounds and their handlers who made a foray into Strathardle which was the territory of the Reid-Robertsons of Straloch and their kindred. A storm blew up and they paused to shelter at Moulin which allowed word to flash ahead of them. The hunted Macgregors were near Kindrogan, a short way south of Straloch, and they were carried up the hill above to avoid leaving a scent trail to their hiding place. The Campbells arrived and were greeted with wary but generous hospitality by the head of the community, a kinsman of the laird of Straloch. The hounds were shut in an outhouse.

The Campbells supped deep on ale - whisky did not supplant ale until well into the 18th century - and their host suggested they slept by the big fire in his house and, it being an inclement night, he would collect plaids from his neighbours to keep them warm. They could go to sleep and he would feed the dogs with the remains of supper. The invaders settled down and their host sent up the hill for the Macgregors' plaids, wrapped them carefully round the snoring Campbells and piled up the scraps from their meal inside the door. Outside again, he chatted to the sentry and suggested that the precious hounds would be better off by the fire than in a barn and so the beasts were moved into the house.

The hounds found their supper, ate it and then found the Campbells, well-packaged as drunken Macgregors, and decided to have them for dessert. The ensuing battle left none of the dogs alive and severely damaged the Campbells who wielded their dirks indiscriminately, deciding that their enemies were upon them. In the morning the sorry Campbells tried to demand a Christian burial for their hounds but were hurried on their way by their host who warned them that Straloch himself was approaching with a large force to expel them from his country. They never again ventured so far from their own lands to harry the persecuted clan.

However the Macgregors continued to be oppressed by the Campbells and continued to be sheltered by the Clan Donnachaidh. In 1589 Sir Duncan Campbell of Glenorchy complained to the Privy Council that his commission against Clan Gregor was frustrated by Duncan Robertson in Struan and Alexander Robertson, heir to Faskally, and these men failed to appear in Edinburgh to answer the charges and were denounced.

The turmoil in Atholl was mirrored in the larger political landscape. Queen Mary, freshly widowed, arrived in Scotland in 1561. In 1566 Darnley, her new husband, was assassinated in Edinburgh and this triggered her downfall. More peacefully the Chronicle of Fortingall states that Robert Robertson of Struan died at Invervack that year and was buried at the church of Struan. In a unique tribute it says 'He was good to those under him, did nothing unjustly, wronged no one, he was a blessing to all his own, and was held at great esteem among his neighbours. I therefore pray that he shall be safe, and so do I think because it is written, *Proximus ille Deo qui scit ratione tacere.*' (He is close to God who knows when to keep quiet).

Chapter Seven
Civil Wars and Montrose

Robert's eldest son William became Chief, the 8th, and he, like his namesake and predecessor, almost led his line to disaster. He married a daughter of Sir Robert Menzies of Weem and appears to have run up such debts to his father-in-law that he was forced to make over more than half his property to him. This was illegal - a feudal delinquency.

In such unsettled times the great men signed bonds of mutual protection, which - in a constantly shifting network of alliances, treachery and violence - were sometimes adhered to. The Reids of Straloch signed one in 1508 with the Earl of Huntly who managed a brief toehold in Atholl when both the Garth Stewarts and Struan were at odds with authority. Both Struan and Lude had bonds with the Earl of Atholl later in the century and in 1584 Struan signed one with Sir Duncan Campbell of Glen Orchy, as well as with Huntly in 1586. Amongst the Lude papers, dated 1568 at Dunkeld, is a Bond between the Earl of Athol and those of the 'surname of Clan Donoquhy' in which both parties agree to protect the other against 'whatsoever persons'. This pact was renewed in 1583

William died childless in 1588, said in one account to have been murdered, and his brother Donald succeeded. His eldest son Robert, by a daughter of Stewart of Foss, became chief in his turn but when he tried to confirm his charters the Crown forfeited the estate because of his uncle's delinquency. However a difference still existed between the letter of the charters and practice. Whatever the law might say, the chief of the Clan still lived on his lands surrounded by his henchmen and received rents from his Clansmen. It would have taken an army to alter the situation and it would be more than a century before armies could venture into the Clan's fastness without enormous difficulty. But without a charter the chief was vulnerable.

Happiness was fully restored in 1600 when Robert received back the lands lost by his uncle. Like so much of the Clan history at this period, some mystery is attached to this. John Robertson was a rich

Edinburgh burgess and kinsman of the chief. Their precise relationship and the source of John's fortune is unknown but he bought the estates from the Crown and gifted them to Struan in a charter. It is likely that the same John Robertson was the builder of 'a small house for the reception of lepers' in Edinburgh in 1591.

The 11th Chief, Alexander, died young in 1636. His son and namesake succeeded as a minor. His were the times of the civil wars. When a chief was a minor, his interests were protected and his followers led by his guardian or Tutor. The Tutor of Struan was his uncle Donald.

Signature of Alexander Robertson of Struan, 12th Chief.

In 1644, the conflict between Charles I - his father James VI of Scotland had inherited the English throne in 1603 and become James I of Great Britain - and the London parliament allied to the Scots Committee of Estates, was raging. In April the Tutor led 800 of the Clan to join the Marquis of Huntly who had raised the Royal standard in the north. He was ordered to assault the town of Montrose and his men 'did brave service with their short guns'. The Scots parliament declared him guilty of high treason.

In July Alastair McColla, a Macdonald chieftain from Ireland, who had been given a commission by the king to invade Argyll and the property of its anti-royalist earl, landed in Scotland with a ferocious army of some 800 northern Irish clansmen. Seizing his chance to ravage the territory of the hated Campbells, McColla laid waste the lands he crossed. Argyll gathered his clan and forced him north. Whether royalist or anti-royalist nobody wanted so many savage warriors living off their land. In the face of the Grants and Mackenzies who were mustering to counter his approach, McColla

James Graham, Marquis of Montrose.

turned towards Atholl. It so happened that the Earl of Atholl was also a minor and so the Clan placed themselves under the Tutor's command, as did all the Stewarts and the other vassals of the earldom. Not for the first time, or the last, the Clan Donnachaidh would fight as the most important component of the Athollmen and they gathered at Truidh just to the north of Lude house to defend their country.

Meanwhile the Earl (later Marquis) of Montrose with a general's commission from the king had come north incognito to avoid the parliamentary forces. He had taken shelter with Patrick Graham of Inchbrackie, brother-in-law of the Tutor, at Tullybelton on the edge of Atholl. Montrose heard what was happening a few miles north and hurried to intervene. Just as the two armies were preparing for conflict, he interceded and persuaded McColla and the Tutor to unite under his banner and fight for the king. There followed one of the most remarkable campaigns in British history.

Leaving John Robertson of Inver holding Blair Castle, Montrose and his army marched south. They brushed by Castle Menzies whose ancient chief made a foolish sortie against them. The party was captured and the octogenarian Menzies died of his wounds. Montrose's 2,000 men first routed an army of 7,000 outside Perth. The Tutor's brother, Duncan Mor of Drumachuine, ancestor of the chief today, intervened to prevent the city being sacked before the victors moved towards Dundee. The Earl of Argyll brought his army from the west to counter this, harrying Atholl on his way through. Montrose defeated him at Fyvie and, to the delight of McColla, moved back through Atholl into Campbell country. The royalists burned their way down Loch Tay, causing £60,000 of damage, and then slaughtered their way across Argyll before retreating into the Great Glen with the earl's battle-hardened army in pursuit. To the north at Inverness Lord Seaforth with his Mackenzies waited to do battle against the royalists. Behind them at Inverlochy, just north of the later-established Fort William, were the Campbells. Montrose was caught between the two armies.

It was January 1645, the Highlands were locked in frost and deep snow. Montrose led his men on a 36-hour march across the toughest and highest stretch of country in Britain to appear from behind Ben Nevis and surprise the Campbells with a dawn attack. The Campbell clansmen on the right wing were used to traditional warfare, fighting as individuals within a brawling mob. McColla had invented the Highland Charge. The royalists ran forward, fired their guns at the edge of their range, then threw themselves on the ground to avoid the returning volley. Abandoning their muskets, they then leapt to their feet and, splitting into wedges of about a dozen men, burst through the shroud of powder smoke into the enemy whilst they struggled to reload.

The Campbell warriors had no answer to this and they crumbled. Their collapse affected the rest of Argyll's army. The Earl was safely in his galley in Loch Linnhe, but his men fled. In the battle and the pursuit 1,500 men including 40 Campbell barons were slain. Montrose is said to have lost eight men killed and only 200 wounded.

Constable's Miscellany, published in 1828, states that after the battle, McColla 'was anxious to learn the name of the smith who has so distinguished himself (he had killed 19 of the enemy), but he, with native modesty, replied that it was not worthy to be named among the many brave men that had fought there that day, but, on being further pressed gave his name as Duncan Robertson and jocularly remarked that he was a 'tinker'. The General thereupon observed Would to God Athole-men had all been tinkers this day! The descendants of this hero, many of whom live in Athole and Rannoch, are to this day marked and distinguished from the rest of the vast population of Robertsons inhabiting that district, by the additional name or epithet of *"N gow chaird"*, that is the family of the tinker smith.'

Montrose won another three major battles, each time utterly defeating a new army thrown against him by the Committee of Estates. Each time the Athollmen were pivotal to his victory. In fact one 19th century Perthshire historian, Robert Scott Fittis, wrote 'The Robertsons of Athole were long esteemed the best swordsmen in

Scotland, and their prowess, under the royal banner, mainly contributed to the brilliant triumphs of Montrose.' A Robertson of Lude once cut off the two buttons on his adversary's shirt collar as a hint his head might follow.

The Athollmen were not present at the battle of Philiphaugh. Montrose lost. He and McColla escaped but the Irish Macdonalds and their women, for Highland armies - indeed all armies - travelled with an immense tail of baggage, stores, spares, wives, children, whores and girlfriends, were exterminated. The Athollmen fought once more before disbanding, at Callander in February 1646 when 700 charged 1200 Campbells who fled with the loss of 80 killed.

In 1650, the words of the Red Book MS, 'when the Royal cause was revived General Middleton gave him (The Tutor) a fresh commission to 'raise and command all the able-bodied men in Atholl, Strathairdle, Glenshee, the Laird of Garntully's lands, the Bishoprick of Dunkeld and the Stormont except those of Clan Cameron and the name of Mcgregor. The levies of these countries were to form but one regiment of which Donald is empowered by his commission to appoint all the Officers.'

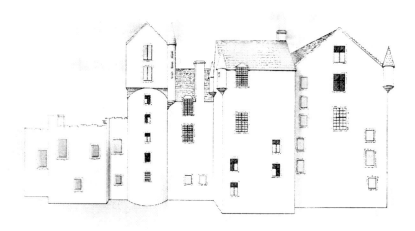

Blair Castle in 1736.

After parliament's victory, an abortive rebellion against the iron grip of Oliver Cromwell, the Lord Protector - one of the more agreeable euphemisms for a dictator - came in 1653 with Glencairn's Rising. Skirmishing took place in Dunkeld but the only recorded casualty from the Clan was one Captain Robertson. Not for the first time, nor for the last, the government in Edinburgh realised that the warrior culture north of the Highland Line was a source of instability for the state. As one official publication stated 'Those gentlemen of Atholl, consisting of the name of Robertson and Stewart, if any be wronged, they all participate.' The parliamentary troops came north and built a chain of forts the length of the Great Glen. On the edge of Atholl they garrisoned Grantully Castle and then Blair. At Invervack, Struan's castle was destroyed, as was Lude. Garth Castle was made ruinous.

The Tutor received a letter of thanks from the King, who would give a pension to the old warrior when the throne was restored in 1660.

'Charles R. Trustie and well beloved, we greet you weill as we heirtofore received frequent and ample testimonie of your great fidelitie and Loyaltie to our blessed Father and self, and your suffering for the same, the bearer hereof Generall Major William Drummond has given us a full account of the continuance and constancie of the same affection and courage in you towards us and our service for which we have thought fitt to return you our Prinslie thanks and acceptation and to assure you that when God shall inable us, we will reward your faithfull services and repair your sufferings, we know weill wee need not encourage you to use your outmost power and credit to assist those who are intrusted by us to conduct our affairs then and who we hope with God's blessing will be the instruments to redeem your countrie from the oppression tyranny and slavery it now groans under what we have done and intend in person to do towards it you will understand by the bearer who will likeways tell you the good opinion we have of you and so we bid you fairwell. Given at Chantilly the 31st October 1653 the fyfth year of our reigne. Directed thus To our trustie and weill beloved. The Tutor of Strowan.'

A glimpse of the character and the touchy honour of one of the chiefs comes in 1681. Alexander, the 12th of Struan held some of his lands from the newly elevated Marquis of Atholl by a decreet of the Court of Session, the highest legal authority in the land, but when his servant, John Fleming, pointed this out 'Struan broke out on Fleming with passionate violence, calling him rascal, knave and villain. He would see the Marquis hanged before he would be his vassal. And as for the Court of Session, he cared not a snuff for its decreet. Then thrusting his hand under the breast of his upper coat, where his dirk and pistol are secretly kept, he said he did not know what held his hand from writing his case on Fleming's skin.' Struan was imprisoned and had to crave pardon from the Privy Council and the Marquis on his knees.

This Alexander built sawmills to exploit the Black Wood of Rannoch 'to the great benefit and conveniency of the country adjacent, besides the keeping of many persons at work'. Much of the timber he floated down from Loch Rannoch via Loch Tummel to the Tay and this was often stolen by 'broken men' - those without land and the protection of their clan. Struan was given permission to build roads into Strathtay as an alternative route for his timber and the Privy Council issued a stern edict against the bandits.

With the restoration of the monarchy in 1660, the political balance tilted again. Atholl was in the ascendant and the Earl of Argyll lost his head which ended up on the same spike once occupied by Montrose. His successor refused to swear to the Test Act in 1681 which gave the king supremacy over both church and state, was declared a traitor and went into exile.

In 1684 the Marquis of Atholl was appointed Lord Lieutenant and Sheriff of Argyll in his place and was ordered by the Privy Council in Edinburgh to take an army west to occupy Inveraray. This time the local war leader was a Stewart, Patrick of Ballechin, known as Patrick of the Battles. His neighbour Robertson of Killiechangie and Baron Reid of Straloch joined with their men. The Marquis left Ballechin in charge and returned home.

The following year the king died. His Roman Catholic brother James II of Great Britain and VII of Scotland succeeded to the throne and his illegitimate nephew, the Duke of Monmouth, landed in southern England to raise a Protestant revolt. He failed and lost his head but the Earl of Argyll came to Scotland to bring out his clan in support. Atholl hurried back west with more troops including Robertson of Faskally's contingent.

Campbell bashing was already a traditional pastime for the Athollmen. They scattered Argyll's army and hanged seventeen of his lairds from the walls of Inveraray. The Marquis, charmed by the gardens round the Earl's residence, uprooted some 35,000 trees and took them home with him. The Earl himself was captured and executed in Edinburgh.

Chapter Eight
Alexander, 13th of Struan

The pendulum swung once more. James VII of Scotland and II of England was Roman Catholic which was grudgingly tolerated until he produced a Catholic heir in 1688. William of Orange, a Protestant married to James's daughter Mary, was invited to take the throne as joint sovereign with his wife and James fled to France. The new regime was endorsed by the parliaments in both London and Edinburgh but many Scots, particularly Highlanders, would not accept the removal of their ancient royal line. They were called Jacobites, the followers of James - Jacobus in Latin. Viscount Dundee led a rebellion and Blair Castle with its stranglehold over the main route into the Highlands, became the key.

The Clan Donnachaidh chief died in November that year. Robert, his only son by his first wife, was a soldier in the Dutch service under the protection of a kinsman Lord Portmore and had come to England with William. He died of ague in the south within a few weeks of his father. His second son was originally destined for the Church and was at St Andrews University where he distinguished himself by winning the silver arrow for archery once awarded to Montrose. Now he became the 13th Chief, Alexander.

His mother, old chief's second wife and daughter of General Baillie of Torwood, was suspected locally of having a hand in Robert's convenient death to ensure Alexander's succession. It was 'a tradition of Rannoch, that as often as she went abroad to ride or walk the crows followed after her in great numbers making a hideous croaking, as if upbraiding her with her guilt'. Alexander never married. The reason he gave was 'that nothing descended of his mother could prosper'.

This doughty lady wrote to the leading Clansmen asking them to discourage her son from becoming involved in any rebellion, but Calvine had already urged him to return home and take command of the Clan. So she sent copies of both letters to Lord Murray at Blair Castle asking him to discount any rebellious behaviour from her son and 'impute it to childesnes'. She asked that her contact with Murray be kept secret from the Clan 'for they will kill me.'

She was wasting her time. Struan, no more than 19, 'hindered the Prince of Orange's declaration being read, beating out his fellow students with a troop of horse being sent by Lord Crawford, whereby he was the first that appeared in the King's service.' When he heard of Dundee's arrival in Atholl he sped back to raise the Clan, succeeding too late for the battle.

At Killiecrankie 3,000 men died when the rebels, mainly Macdonalds, Camerons and McLeans, swept a redcoat army into the river Garry. But the rebel leader was killed and he was irreplaceable. His successor Colonel Cannon dispatched Struan and his followers towards Perth to harry the retreating government troops. General Mackay and a body of dragoons who had missed the battle fell on them and are said to have killed 150 Clansmen and captured 30 others. Struan retreated to join the rest of the rebels now besieging Dunkeld but they were beaten back. The Rising fizzled out although Struan and a couple of score of his inclination remained as a mounted cavalry troop commanded by Cannon and were the last to surrender.

Alexander was captured but managed to escape to France to join his 'misfortunate master', King James. His estates were forfeited in 1690 and for thirteen years he remained in exile and is said to have served and campaigned in the French army.

With the accession of Queen Anne in 1703, he obtained a pardon and returned home. An MS of 1834 says 'He entered into his estate, and soon rendered himself exceedingly popular, particularly among his own

John Graham, Viscount Dundee.

Clan and tenants, to whom he ever was an indulgent master. He entered deeply into the intrigues for the restoration of the exiled Royal family, and strongly opposed the Union with England in 1707.

'From this period down to 1714 his exertions on behalf of the Royal Family continued unabated. What rendered him most obnoxious, if not most dangerous, to the opposite party, were his political writings. These poetical squibs and diatribes obtained the most unbounded popularity among the Scottish Jacobites of the period. What perhaps enhanced their value, was the difficulty of procuring them, for owing to the high political seasoning they contained they could not safely be published. It is certain that his poetical talents made Strowan's name familiar among his contemporaries, and the use he made of them joined to his consideration as a Chief at the head of a devoted and numerous Clan, and his activity as a politician, rendered him as valuable to the Jacobites, as he was dangerous to the Whigs.'

Struan's sister, Mrs Margaret Robertson, was a staunch supporter of her brother, determined to do her best to preserve the Clan lands and the dignity of the family, but her brother treated her very shabbily. A spinster, for her title of Mistress referred to her sex rather than her marital condition, she inherited an income from the estate but he refused to pay it. She went to law and 'the officer employed to put the writ in execution was accompanied to Rannoch by fifty men, under the command of Stewart of Tulloch, and by Mrs Margaret in person. They were informed by the servants at his residence of Mount Alexander [Dunalastair], that Strowan was living at Carie, eight miles farther up the country, and they proceeded there accordingly, leaving Mrs Margaret at the village of Kinloch Rannoch, situated half-way between Carie and the Mount. Upon arriving at Carie, they perceived the laird with his red cloak and hat, and carrying a gold headed cane, walking in a stately manner, alone, on the lawn before the house. The party, happy at the prospect of accomplishing their duty so easily, instantly rushed upon him, but alas, when they laid hands on this imposing figure they found under the red cloak and hat not the laird of Strowan, but a bare-legged ghillie. Meantime, the laird, who had been very nearly surprised, hastened through the wood behind the house to Loch Rannoch, accompanied by the twelve men who were always about his person, took boat, and rowed directly to the village of Kinloch, where Mrs

Margaret waited for the messenger and his party. He instantly apprehended the unfortunate lady and carried her to a small island, where she was put under confinement.'

Alexander, the 13th Chief.

Lord Portmore was descended from the Robertsons of Dulcaben. He had made a career in Holland and been ennobled by King William. He joined with the Duke of Atholl to push for her freedom but the poor lady was marooned for fifteen months until she made her own escape and returned home. Only the advent of the next Jacobite Rising led by the Earl of Mar in September 1715 kept her brother from confining her again.

Struan joined Mar in Perth with 300 men and he was sent to Castle Campbell, some fourteen miles south of Crieff, to 'clear the country of the enemy, cut off their parties, and confine them to their garrison.'

Castle Menzies.

'In the end of October he surprised and took the garrison in the Castle of Weem (Castle Menzies), belonging to the Whig family of Menzies of Weem, secured the persons of several of the Whig gentlemen in that district, and procured plentiful provisions for the Highland Army. ' (Most of the castle garrison was absent when the Clan attacked, drinking at the adjacent inn). Mar, in a letter dated 30th October, notes Struan's Brigade, consisting of from 400 to 500 men, as the strongest in the army.

At the Battle of Sheriffmuir on 13th November, the Clan Regiment fought on the left wing. Struan charged too far and was briefly captured by a party of dragoons. His men missed him and charged back to the rescue just as he surrendered and was in the act of giving away his purse to a trooper. 'The trooper turned on his heel and called out "Your purse by right is mine". "Yes it is", said the laird, "pray come back for it", but the fellow shook his head, and ran off.' Alexander discovered this man's name, and afterwards sent the purse containing sixty guineas to him at Carlisle.

The battle was indecisive, the Rising collapsed and Struan was taken prisoner. 'A party of soldiers who were conveying him to the Castle of Edinburgh halted for the night at Amulree. His sister, the ill-used Mrs Margaret, or as he himself always called her, Black Margaret, arrived there soon after under a fictitious name. (Alexander himself was once described as 'a little black man') She went into the room where the soldiers sat, congratulated them upon the good service they had done in apprehending the arch traitor Strowan, charged them to take good care that he should not escape, and distributed money among them, telling them at the same time that she had ordered the landlord to supply them with liquor. As she had anticipated, all the men got drunk, and her brother found no difficulty in effecting his escape. In the morning when the prisoner was missed Mrs Margaret gave the men a severe reprimand for their negligence, but she was shrewdly suspected of the plot notwithstanding this pretence of zeal for the Hanoverian interest, though she was never called to account for it.'

Struan escaped to Holland in the summer of 1716 and rejoined the exiled royal court. Meantime Margaret went to London to lobby King George for the return of the estates. She made such a nuisance of herself 'that he at last exclaimed in a transport of impatience, "For God's sake, give that woman back her lands and let me have peace."' The estate was restored to her in 1723 and Struan returned home in 1726, although he did not get a pardon until 1731.

'There is a tradition in Rannoch that Strowan's pardon was sent to him through General Wade, a gentleman for whom, notwithstanding his politics, he had great value and with whom, though they had not then met, he corresponded in regard to the military roads and bridges constructed under Wade's charge. (Wade had been sent north to subdue the clans by building roads so that troops and cannon could enter the Highlands. A great bon viveur, he made himself popular amongst the very men who should have been his most bitter enemies. His masterpiece was the bridge at Aberfeldy, built in 1730, and for this Struan provided timber for scaffolding from the Black Wood. The Chief also penned a fulsome poem in praise of Wade when the bridge was opened.)

'The General appointed Strowan to meet him in Badenoch on a certain day to receive the pardon, but as the laird was journeying northward for that purpose he chanced to meet a number of his friends at the Inn of Dalnacardoch, where he entertained them according to his custom. The jovial party forgot General Wade, the pardon, and everything connected with it, for a full week, and at the end of that period Strowan proceeded on his journey. The General asked him how he could trifle with his safety in a matter of such importance. "Because", returned he with his characteristic politeness, "I felt assured that the pardon was as safe in General Wade's keeping as in mine."

'From this time forward General Wade and Strowan were on very friendly terms. The General frequently urged him to make an unqualified submission to King George, and to take the oath to his Government; and on one occasion, when Strowan was complaining to him of the annoyance he received from Mrs Margaret's creditors, Wade said, "If you will accompany me to London, and allow me to present you at Court, I will engage that all your troubles shall be at an end, simply upon your kissing the King's hand." Strowan's well known answer cannot be repeated here; but it is needless to say that it was a decided negative to the General's proposition.'

General George Wade.

The estates carried debts but Struan ignored them and eventually a warrant was issued for his arrest. 'A Messenger-at-Arms, with a Sheriff's posse of about thirty men, proceeded to Rannoch to put the warrant in execution. The party was met by some of Strowan's men upon the Banks of the River Tummel, a few miles below his seat of Mount Alexander. Their papers and arms were taken from them, and they themselves beaten, bruised and maltreated, and finally thrown into the deep and rapid Tummel "to the danger of their lives and great hurt and prejudice of their persons". The Messenger states that Strowan caused his papers to be returned to him at Perth, but that he, "the said Strowan Robertson, kept the aforesaid arms, illegally and masterfully taken off the persons of the Complainer and his assistants, as said is".

'Another Messenger and party, who went afterwards to serve an Indictment upon Strowan and his Tenants for this breach of the peace, met with no better success than their predecessors, for they in their turn were used with the same violence and stripped of their arms and papers.'

'At last, James Robertson of Blairfettie, himself one of the creditors, and, as a Highlander, somewhat better qualified to contend against these masterful courses, took upon him the hazardous office of Factor; but we soon find him complaining to the Court that Strowan with a strong party of armed followers proceeded to collect the rents, turn out tenants, let farms, and to exercise every other act of proprietary in defiance of their Lordships' commission. "He disdains", says the Petitioner, "to submit to the laws, and opposes all law and authority." The Complainer farther states that no Messenger would venture into Strowan's country, unless he was attended by a military force; and that the factor himself lived in great hazard of his life.

Division ruins State, and private Men
Their Fate is hard who are Divided, Then
What must he do whose Cause is really good
When overpower'd by Offspring of his Blood?
'Tis thought he should oppose such insollence
And make their Purse feel their want of Sense
By this in time he will their Strength bring down
Retaining as before his Rightful Own

Verse written by Struan when
sued by Blairfettie.

Donald Robertson of Woodsheal, a cousin of Blairfettie, challenged the unfortunate factor to single combat for the affront he had put upon his chief by accepting the obnoxious trust. They fought with broadswords, and as Strowan wrote to Woodsheal's brother, "Blairfettie was sent home a cripple".

'In 1745 Strowan was himself too old and infirm to take an active share in the campaign under Prince Charles; but he sent a party of his Clan under Woodsheal, and another party followed led Robertson of Drumachuine, his heir male, with whom he unfortunately lived on bad terms. The Robertsons did not muster so strongly upon this occasion as in 1715, when Strowan himself was in the prime and vigour of his age, and marched at their head. He went as far as Dalnacardoch, to meet the Prince on his way south. When he was presented, he said: "Sir, I devoted my youth to the service of your grandfather, and my manhood to that of your father, and now I am come to devote my old age to your Royal Highness". Charles, well acquainted with his history, folded the old man in his arms, and wept. He accompanied the Highland Army to Edinburgh, but his infirmities had increased to such a degree, that he was obliged to return home after the Battle of Prestonpans, leaving his Clan under the charge of Woodsheal and Drumachuine.

'It is said that no overt act of treason could be proved on this occasion against Strowan, and therefore that he was allowed to retain possession of his estate, but as he had publicly joined the Highland Army the forbearance of the Government may rather be attributed to the good offices of General Wade and other friends, and to his extreme old age, which would not allow him to give further disturbance to the Government. The Laird of Blairfettie having been engaged in the Rebellion was incapacitated from further interference in Strowan's matters, so that, for the brief period of life that remained to him, the old gentleman enjoyed peace and quietness. He died at Carie on April 28th, 1749, in the 80th year of his age.' He was the only man in Britain to take part in all three of the great Jacobite Risings - 1689, 1715 and 1745.

Chapter Nine

The Poet Chief

'The room in which Strowan slept and entertained company at Carie was the factor's kitchen in 1770' reads an account of Alexander at home. 'In the garden, which had once had a good wall, besides fruit trees, might be spied mint, rhubarb, and flowers in their natural state, monuments of their former master's taste and attention. He lived constantly in thatched houses of one storey, the family ones having been burnt in times of war. At a time when his great neighbours at Dunkeld and Taymouth had no notion of pleasure ground or gardening, he planned, and in part executed a villa at Mount Alexander with much taste and judgement, being picturesque even when deserted and overrun with bushes and weeds. And his garden at Carie was one of the best in the country and planted with good trees, both for shade and fruit. Between these two places he divided his time as the fancy struck him; and it was but four miles betwixt them.

'James Moray of Abercairny said that between 1720 and 1730 he used to go over and stay a week with Strowan, who was his relation, and always very kind to him. Nothing he said could be more brilliant and delightful than that gentleman's wit, or more pertinent than his remarks upon men and things. But the pleasure of his guests was diminished by the style of dissipation in which he lived. In the morning his common potation was whisky and honey, and when inclined to take what he termed a meridian, brandy and sugar were called for. These were the liquors which he generally used, not being able to afford wines, and perhaps liking spirits better. When his guests declined the beverage, he would say good naturedly, "If you be not for it, I am." Besides taking too much of these cordials, he exhausted his spirit by lively talk; on these occasions he would turn into his bed, which stood in the room where he ate and drank. After sobering himself with a nap, he got up and walked abroad, till he had recourse again to his cups.

'None was fonder of a visit from Strowan than James, Duke of Athole, whose social hours were joyous and dignified; who lived with his vassals like a parent and a companion. It had been the custom for every gentleman to kiss the Duchess. He learned from her woman that one of Strowan's companions (afterwards an officer in the French service) had once been his menial servant. On her complaining of having to salute such a man, the Duke archly answered 'Madam, my friend is a greater man than the king, for he can both make and unmake a gentleman when he pleases.'

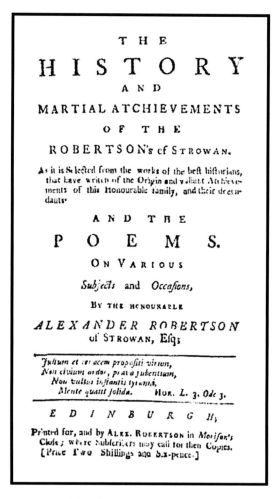

The first printed history.

'In his time Rannoch was the seat of numerous and daring gangs of thieves. As they bade defiance to the government, it was not in

Strowan's power to repress them, though he abominated their courses. Being told of a great thief on his estate, he said he would try his honesty, affecting not to believe the charge, whereupon he dispatched him to Perth for a sixpence loaf, which the man did with great dispatch, bringing with him a roll, which was then given into the bargain. As he might have concealed it, Strowan would never after hear anything wrong of a man of so much honour.'

After the chief's death, his valet and the executor of his estate, Charles Alexander, gathered together his manuscripts and published them in Edinburgh in an unauthorised book of poems that had wide circulation. It was republished about 1803 along with a short history of the family. Of these works one Clansman wrote in 1821 'the one formerly published by the footman or valet of the late Strowan so miserable & incorrect that it is a disgrace to have such an account of the clan in circulation'.

The volume contains epitaphs, political diatribes, odes, translations of Latin and Greek poets, parodies and short humorous verse but sprinkled amongst them are verses of startling bawdiness. His friends were horrified; such material was the product of dissipated revelling and should never have been printed, but destroyed to preserve the old man's reputation. This certainly suffered and it is rare to find a complete volume of the book since most copies had the naughty bits torn out to preserve the tender sensibilities of the Victorian era.

His love of nature and his Hermitage at Mount Alexander is very evident in two poems to Argentinius that he wrote. The Argentine Well with its water silvered with flecks of mica, still lies down the hill to the east of the ruined mansion house now on the site. He wrote a lament when he left to go into exile and a Hymn on his return, a few verses which are below. Strephon is the writer himself.

The HYMN of ARGENTINUS on STRUAN'S Return to the Hermitage.

Expand thy Gates, thou bless'd Abode!
Thy long neglected Cells repair.
Confess the bounteous Care of God,
Our STREPHON breathes his native Air:

Lo! he returns to cheer our dismal State,
And purify once more his sweet, his lov'd Retreat.
Ere while we mourn'd, with honest Grief,
STREPHON, just Object of our Tears,
Our Swains in Sighing sought Relief,
Our Nymphs in silent Floods of Tears:
Our callow Shepherds, in a doleful Mood,
Like Orphans dwindled, and despair'd of Food.

But now they congregate to sing
Te Deums with distended Throats;
The woody Rocks, disused to sing,
Repeat with Joy the heav'nly Notes,
And bless the great Creator, who displays
His secret Providence in wondrous Ways.

Our pretty feather'd Quire apace,
In shady Bow'rs commence to build,
And propagate a num'rous Race,
Fearing no more to be expell'd,
Like STREPHON, in their Mansions to remain
Obscure, till Innocence revive her drooping Train.

The other end of the spectrum could be represented by the following verse:

LIBERTY PRESERVED: OR, LOVE DESTROYED.

At length the Bondage I have broke
Which gave me so much Pain;
I've slipt my Heart out of the Yoke,
Never to drudge again;
And conscious of my long Disgrace,
Have thrown my Chain at Cupid's Face.

If ever he attempts again
My freedom to enslave,
I'll court the Godhead of Champain

Which makes the Coward brave,
And, when the Deity has heal'd my Soul,
I'll drown the little Bastard in my Bowl.

The chief's poetry has not stood the test of time. It is not included in anthologies and no academic has evaluated his work although a delightful quote ends such an attempt by the minister of Little Dunkeld in 1820. 'I endeavoured to shew that a poet long consigned to oblivion deserves to be remembered and it is probable that this poetic chief had no idea that that task should be performed by a presbyterian.' Jacobites, almost without exception, were Roman Catholic or Episcopalian whose ministers would not swear loyalty to King George. The clergyman tiptoes round the obscenities describing them as merely 'the offspring of negligence, of vexation or of resentment which he himself would have consigned to oblivion, for he was too much a gentleman to offend either morals, delicacy or refined taste.' It is this author who states 'Lewis [Louis of France] XIV pronounced him the most accomplished Gentleman in his court. Indeed he went under the name of the Scottish Gentleman.'

David Stevenson of St Andrews University writing in 2000, described many of such works as political. 'Bawdy and obscenity were useful as assaults on establishment values, as proclaiming commitment to libertinism through sexual explicitness, and as propaganda weapons to be employed in the Jacobite cause.' In attacking King William, for example, the chief accuses him of homosexuality, highlighting his childlessness and ignoring his stable of mistresses. One fragment comes already censored. King James was a manly fellow but 't'other underperforming puny prig, Could only with his Page retire and fr[**]'

Another commentator wrote that 'the fatal fault of the book is not that it contains some bad poems, but that it does not contain any good ones...the merit of the verses is that they give up a reflection of the best side of the author's character - his courage, his steadfastness, and his stoical yet cheerful endurance of whatever fortune might befall. It is impossible to read them without getting a better understanding of the man, and conceiving a higher respect for him...Strowan's personality is much more interesting than his poems. Judged by strict literary canons he was merely a Highland laird who, with some facility for rhyming but no poetic power, wrote verses in imitation of the Restoration poets. Estimated, however, by the totality of his character and career, he stands as a singular example of nobility and fortitude, essentially unharmed by some degrading traits and circumstances, and it is because he could not help giving sometimes an air of nobility even to his doggerel that his poems may still be read with interest.'

In 1749 two thousand men - women did not attend funerals - followed his coffin from Carie fifteen miles to Struan kirk where he was buried amid the dust of his ancestors. As well as mourning the passing of the old chief, they were mourning the passing of an era and, perhaps, the devastating blows the Clan had suffered during his lifetime.

The Poet Chief was obviously a difficult man for those close to him. To balance his charm, one suspects he must have possessed a strong streak of irresponsibility and selfishness. His treatment of his sister as described was lamentable, and thought so by his contemporaries. He also failed to maintain relationships with important cadet families of the Clan. His disagreements with James Robertson of Blairfettie are outlined above and he was no lightweight, being described as one of the best officers in the rebel army in 1745 by Lord George Murray, its most capable general.

The chief also took against his own heirs. His younger brother Duncan had become, like his older half brother, a soldier of fortune in Lord Portmore's regiment in the Dutch army of William of Orange - a betrayal in the eyes of his sibling - and died in 1718. Duncan's son Robert, a great favourite with his uncle, was killed in a duel, 'fairly done' with a Lachlan Maclean in Cahors in southern France. Struan wished to change the succession to his niece, Sybilla, and fell out with the next male heir, his cousin Alexander of Drumachuine and his son Duncan. In fact the estate had been owned by Margaret and Struan only had the rents for his lifetime. After that it went according to Margaret's will and that was to the male heir Drumachuine. Fortunately Struan had not the cash to go to law on the matter. Had he won, the Clan would share a chief with the Macdonells of Glengarry.

Struan could muster 300 men from his lands, but 500 of his Clan were vassals of others and many of them also fought for the Jacobites. In the Rising of 1715 George Robertson of Faskally with his royal charter dating from 1504 and an extensive estate from Bruar to Pitlochry commanded his own little regiment of vassals at Sheriffmuir and many other Clansmen fought in the two Atholl battalions. The Murrays, whose ancestor had married the daughter of the last Stewart Earl, were now dukes and the head of this family held close to the government from which his power ultimately derived, but younger brothers often joined the rebels. The Atholl Brigade was part of the detachment led by MacIntosh of Borlum. They crossed the Forth, held off the government army from Leith Citadel before marching across the Scottish border, believing that many thousands of English Jacobites would join them and carry on to London. They met instead the redcoats and were besieged at Preston about 60 miles south of Carlisle. They surrendered on November 14, the day after the fiasco of Sheriffmuir.

EPITAPH on *Robert Robertſon,* Son to Colonel *Duncan Robertſon,* killed in a Duel before he was 19 Years of Age, and buried on the Spot.

the caſk

THIS ſcanty Hillock does incloſe
of Ail the Spirit Youth could loſe,
Which a continued Luſtre gave
To all the Mildneſs Youth could have.

Oh! that his Meekneſs of Deſire
Had got the Aſcendant o'er his Fire;
But too much Life, alas! could bring
Death's rapid and untimely Sting.

Sweet lovely Shade repoſe in Peace,
Tho' laid in this unhallow'd Place;
Thy ſpotleſs Duſt, wherever found,
Makes holy the profaneſt Ground.

Young Reader, here with Pity gaze,
And learn to live out all thy Days.

Written by Struan on his nephew's death.

Alexander Robertson of Drumachuine could have followed his chief but instead he was a captain in the Atholl Brigade and was taken at Preston. Only very rough casualty lists from this Rising exists and it is impossible to calculate the losses to the Clan. The fate of some of those captured at Preston is known. About 200 officers were marched down to London in chains, some were lodged in the Tower, others at Newgate prison. Other prisoners ended up in Chester, Lancaster or Liverpool. There were trials; some had their estates confiscated, others executed, most were transported to North America and sold as indentured servants to work in the plantations for seven years. Drumachuine was sentenced to death. When he was called to the scaffold, his younger brother Donald who had been reprieved answered in his stead. Donald was executed; Drumachuine released.

Chapter Ten

The Rising of 1745

Atholl was comparatively peaceful for the next thirty years. Cattle theft was still a problem. Struan seemed to connive to keep the forces of the law at bay and thus give bandits shelter in Rannoch. But in place of narrow paths through the hills and dangerous fords across the rivers, General Wade had bridged the Tay at Aberfeldy and the Tummel which meant that a passable road now connected Clan country with the Lowlands. Goods could now be carried on carts instead of pack horses and new ideas began to flow through the glens.

Wade's Bridge at Aberfeldy.
Struan wrote a poem on its opening in 1730.

Lowland Scotland, at last, had begun to exploit the benefits of the 1707 Union with England and was making rapid economic progress. But the traditional way of life still clung on in the Highlands and so did traditional attitudes. The first Highland regiment of the British army, the Black Watch, had been formed in 1739 and many of the brightest young Athollmen had joined as ordinary soldiers and received a professional training in arms which they would later put to use in a way the government had not foreseen. The men of the regiment fought their first battle in 1745 at Fontenoy against the French in Flanders and impressed the Duke of Cumberland, King George's son, with their heroism.

Struan's belief in the restoration of the Stuarts was the guiding force of his life. The same could be said for a handful of other local lairds. Some, like Sir Robert Menzies, the chief of his clan, followed his family's century-long policy of favouring the government, as did James, Duke of Atholl whose elder brother William had been disinherited for his Jacobitism. However most of the lairds and most of everyone else wanted no more than to live peacefully and ensure their families were fed. It was all very well for the great men to muster their warriors and go off to fight, but this brought with it the likelihood of some opposing army ravaging the home country - burning houses, crippling cattle, destroying food stores and assaulting the old, the women and the children left unprotected.

Prince Charles.

But a new Stuart prince, reared in the exiled court in Rome, was ready to test his mettle. The French also knew that any Rising against the Hanoverian king would considerably distract the British war effort against them on the Continent. Prince Charles Edward was 24 and a man of charisma and courage, if little ability. In 1744 the French gave him arms and men and he set sail for Scotland. The weather beat them back.

The following year his sponsors would offer him no help and his father, the so-called James VIII and the uninspiring figurehead of the 1715 Rising, forbade him to leave Rome. Nevertheless he found a ship and, in July 1745, was landed in the Hebrides with seven companions amongst whom was the disinherited elder brother of the Duke of Atholl, known as Duke William to the Jacobites to differentiate him from his younger brother who possessed the title and Blair Castle..

The first chiefs he met told him to go home, a rebellion without French support could only end in disaster. One of the 'what-ifs?' of history is the course of the Gaelic and clan culture had this advice been taken. But Charles appealed to Highland honour and the recruits came in.

On August 31st the Jacobite army of some 2,000 Camerons, Macdonalds and Appin Stewarts reached Blair Castle. Duke James had fled south and many of his vassals followed him. The Duke's cousin, the widowed Charlotte Robertson of Lude, acted as hostess to the prince both at the castle and at the ball which she threw at neighbouring Lude House. The people of Atholl flocked to see Charlie - which closely approximates to the pronunciation of the Gaelic for his name 'Tearlach' - but they showed little enthusiasm for joining the cause and returned to their homes. Meanwhile Duke William conferred with his advisers and began recruiting.

George Robertson of Faskally raised his men, as did his vassal Robertson of Calvine. Amongst Clan vassals of the duke, prominent Jacobites included Blairfettie, a veteran of the '15 Rising, who became the trusted major of Lord George Murray's battalion of the Athollmen. Another was Donald Robertson of Woodsheal who was given command of the contingent from Struan's lands when the old man decided he was past soldiering. The government tried to tempt Duncan Robertson of Drumachuine, the chief's heir, to their side by offering him a commission in the Black Watch but he turned it down. He was in poor health when the Prince arrived at Blair and Duke William appointed him governor of Atholl when the Jacobite army marched south. He had recovered to fight at the head of a contingent of the Clan at Culloden.

Another Clan leader was Rob Ban Robertson of Invervack (*ban - fair*). In his sixties when the Prince landed, he had already enjoyed a colourful life, working his way through four wives and gaining his spurs at Sheriffmuir by rescuing Struan when he was taken prisoner.

After a couple of days at Blair, Prince Charles continued his march towards Perth. Duke William stayed behind to gather the fighting men of Atholl before joining the rest of the rebel army. It immediately became apparent that this task would not be easy. It was thirty years since Sheriffmuir, years in which the old Highland way of life in Atholl was in decline.

When a laird was a keen Jacobite, his tenants had no option but to join the rebel ranks. Any fit man between 16-60 must follow his laird or, at best, he and his family would be evicted. Today an equivalent might be being stripped of your possessions and citizenship and deposited at your country's border. But many lairds were ambivalent; some were government supporters - like the Reids of Straloch - and others were too old or too young to fight. In such cases it appears that folk did all they could to avoid the recruiting gangs that Duke William and Drumachuine sent round Atholl. These were not gentle and often consisted of Macphersons who, unhampered by ties of kinship, could threaten to burn cottages and cripple the cattle of those who were reluctant to volunteer.

The difficulties are revealed in the case of Lady Lude. Her son was under age but his mother was described as behaving like a 'light giglet' by Duke James's chamberlain and spy Thomas Bisset in the presence of the handsome prince. (giglet, in Dr Johnson's Dictionary of 1755, is defined as 'a wanton', but one hopes it was already moving towards its later meaning of 'a giddy, laughing girl') She told her tenants that she would set the clans upon them if they did not join the rebels and even threatened to hang them. Nevertheless all save one deserted before the first battle. Faskally had similar problems, though not as severe. Of the 3,000 potential soldiers in Atholl and Rannoch, less than a thousand fought for the Jacobites.

Along with the first contingent of the Atholl Brigade, Struan and his Clansmen marched south. They met up with the rest of their army at camp outside Edinburgh which had already surrendered to the prince.

The Battle of Prestonpans was fought on the 19th September. Struan was present but only as a spectator having accepted that being 74 with a well-pickled liver made him too old to fight. Prince Charles had signed Woodsheal's commission as lieutenant colonel in command of the Clan battalion three days earlier. When the Highlanders charged, the redcoats put up little resistance and turned tail. In the second line the Athollmen scarcely blooded their weapons which was probably just as well since they were poorly armed, in some cases with little more than a sickle blade attached to a pole.

After the battle captured weapons were abundant and Struan returned home. He ordered Woodsheal, 'if they please' to fight with Macdonald of Keppoch but he and his men preferred to amalgamate with their fellow Athollmen. Struan himself with a body of Clansmen under Woodsheal's father, Rob Ban, returned to Rannoch in the defeated general's carriage wearing his wolfskin dressing gown and gold chain and comforted by his barrel of brandy. His powdered chocolate was treated with grave suspicion by the Highlanders and sold as substandard English snuff in Perth. At Tummel Bridge the roads ran out, so the escort detached the wheels and carried the coach and its occupant back to Rannoch.

There is a letter addressed to the old chief by Prince Charles, dated Holyrood House, 31st Oct 1745. 'I write this to let you know that I am perfectly well satisfied with ye service you have already done me as well as with yr zeal to continue to serve in person. But as I am at the same time apprized of yr delicate state of health I think it altogether improper for you to follow me in ye manner you propose, for when once the army moves from hence there will be no safety on the road for travellers like you, and you would endanger yr life and liberty by attempting it. I put too great a value upon them to allow you to venture them in such a manner, and therefore I rather desire you to stop at home where by yr presence and authority you may serve me in another way and be equally assured of the value and friendship I have for you. Charles P.R.'

110 prisoners were marched to Logierait where James Robertson of Killiechangie was deputising for the governor, Drumachuine. He and Robertson of Eastertyre were ordered to feed and house them in the jail

at Logierait from where Rob Roy had once escaped.

The prince's army marched south from Edinburgh and reached Derby. They were only 150 miles from London and there was panic in the capital, but Cumberland had brought 20,000 battle-hardened redcoats over from Flanders and another 40,000 regulars and militia were manoeuvring to corner and destroy the ragged 4,500 rebels. At a Council meeting, the Highland chiefs told the prince that disaster was sure to follow if they did not retreat and, very reluctantly, he agreed.

Lord George Murray

Lord George Murray was younger brother of the Duke of Atholl and by far the best rebel general. He was accused of favouring the Athollmen for they seem to have scarcely fired a shot before the final battle, but he had drilled them himself and considered them the cream of his troops. He was unwilling to squander them unnecessarily. Shadowed by government armies, the Jacobites retreated back into Scotland and, during a downpour on January 17th, met with the confident redcoats. At the battle of Falkirk, Lord George's faith in the Athollmen was justified. The left wing of the government army broke and the other Highland regiments scampered after them through the rain, each man determined to snatch his share of plunder. Three redcoat regiments were still intact and could have commanded the battlefield had it not been for the discipline of the Atholl Brigade. They remained on the rain swept hilltop in their ranks and prevented the victory from becoming a disaster.

The Highlanders continued the retreat north. Blairfettie struggled through Perth and Dunkeld in command of the remnants of the artillery while the bulk of the clan regiments marched through Crieff. One little boy who lived north of Amulree recorded many years later that he heard the sound of bagpipes and ran to look over the farm yard wall and down to the Wade road. There he watched Prince Charlie and regiment after regiment of Highlanders marching past towards Taybridge at Aberfeldy. The prince spent a couple of nights at Castle Menzies, to the great embarrassment of the chief, before moving to Blair. The problems of desertion had not eased, Struan himself was condemned by Drumachuine for allowing deserters to cross the ferry at Kinloch Rannoch and even for entertaining them at Carie.

When redcoats began to probe north of the Highland Line, the retreat continued to Inverness. Atholl was left undefended and soon the Argyll Militia, Campbell clansmen in government pay, moved in to occupy what was rebel territory, usually quartering themselves in the lairds' houses.

A month later Mrs Robertson of Blairfettie smuggled a letter north, telling her husband of the hardships they were enduring under the Campbells and asked for help. On the 12th March, Lord George marched his regiment down from Inverness and launched a spectacular raid. Leaving Dalwhinnie on the evening of the 16th and sweeping through Drumochter Pass in the small hours of the morning, the troops split into thirty-odd small companies each of which attacked the soldiers that occupied their own homes.

In 1790, Mrs Robertson gave an interview in which she described what happened. 'Lady Blairfettie said that there was a garrison in Blairfettie House of about fifty men; that they did no other mischief to her than eating all her provisions, and that she and her children were starving; that she sent a herd boy to her husband, who was at Inverness with the Highlanders, to see if he could give her any redress, and desired the boy to come back immediately. The boy did not return; but four or five nights afterwards, when she was in bed, she was called up by a rap at her room door, and she asked what was wanted. A person, whose voice she knew to be that of one of her servants who had gone off with her husband, answered that Blairfettie was below, and wished to see her immediately. When she went down, she saw the garrison disarmed, and prisoners in the dining-room, and about a dozen of her husband's tenants and servants standing over them with drawn swords. Blairfettie desired her to point out any of the prisoners who had behaved ill to her. She answered she had no complaint but what I have stated; and after remaining four or five days Blairfettie and his men left the house...The house was pillaged after Culloden.'

With scarcely a casualty Atholl was retaken by the Jacobites and hundreds of the captured militia herded north to Ruthven. Lord George then besieged Blair Castle which was occupied by the 21st Regiment under Col Sir Andrew Agnew, a foul-mouthed, foul-tempered old warrior. His opinion of Lord George was succinct. When the rebels began potting cannon balls at the castle, he said 'Is the loon clean daft, knocking down his own brother's house?' Then an urgent recall came from the prince because Cumberland was preparing to cross the river Spey to confront the rebel army.

Chapter Eleven

Culloden and its Aftermath

The battle of Culloden took place on the morning of 16th April 1746. The ground between Nairn and Inverness on Drummossie moor chosen by the prince to make his stand was unsuitable for the Highland style of battle. In addition his army was half-starved, exhausted, outgunned and outnumbered. Their supply system had failed and the Athollmen had been marching all night in an attempted surprise raid on the enemy which had been aborted at dawn.

The men of Clan Donnachaidh fought on the right wing with their neighbours. They endured devastating artillery fire before the Mackintoshes, next in the line, could stand it no longer and charged. The right wing followed. The Athollmens' route ran alongside a wall which sprouted a line of muskets that poured fire into their flank, complementing government artillery firing grapeshot and canister. The redcoat front line broke under the impact of the charge but the second line held and, together with Wolf's Regiment which attacked from the side, they destroyed the Atholl Brigade. The rest of the rebel army was chased from the field.

The following day the remains of the Jacobite force met at Ruthven, some thirty miles to the south, where they disbanded, but precious few Athollmen were amongst them. Most were still lying on the heather at Drummossie moor where the charge had been halted. Twenty two gentlemen of Atholl and neighbourhood are recorded as being killed. Woodsheal was wounded but survived. His brothers Charles and Alexander were killed. His cousin Donald was wounded. Another cousin, James, was killed whilst hiding in the hills after the battle. John Robertson of Wester Bohespic died, as did Duncan Robertson of Calvine and Hugh Reid in Foss, James Robertson of Balnacree and his son, and Trinafour's son. Duncan Robertson of Auchleeks was wounded and was said to be the last man to stop fighting and vacate the battlefield. Blairfettie escaped to France and died there but Woodsheal was allowed to return to Atholl in 1772 and died in 1775. Lady Lude lay low in an Edinburgh lodging house calling herself Mrs Black.

Memorial to the Clans at Culloden.

Of those known to have fought with the Atholl Brigade only seventy five bore surnames of Clan Donnachaidh. The names and fate of most ordinary Clansmen were never recorded since nobody wishes to advertise that they or their relatives fought in a failed rebellion. But in many cases it was obvious for rebel estates had few or no menfolk left.

In the aftermath of Culloden, the redcoats burned, raped, looted and murdered their way through the Highlands uncaring whether or not their victims were involved with the Rising. Atholl and Rannoch escaped comparatively lightly, mainly through the influence of the Thomas Bisset, the duke's chamberlain, who did his best to preserve his master's lands and the people on them. But the Argyll Militia were once again the occupiers and they felt they had scores to settle after the humiliation during March's raid.

'In winter 1746 & spring 1747 all Rannoch was burnt and plundered, and some people were killed by the king's troops. They indeed extended their devastations over all the adjacent valleys without any distinction of friend or foe, the innocent or the guilty. The inhabitants were thus deprived of home & shelter during an inclement season and reduced to wretchedness and despair, and the name of the Duke of Cumberland became associated with every enormity which could excite or deserve the execration of mankind. These facts I had from eye witnesses. Struan's houses in Carie & at Mount Alexander shared the common calamity.' So wrote the minister of Little Dunkeld in 1800.

George Robertson of Faskally famously hid in the oak tree still standing on the outskirts of Pitlochry and thus escaped the searching soldiers. Struan was burnt out of the Hermitage and his Clansmen carried him into the depths of the Black Wood when the redcoats attacked Carie. The harrying of the Highlands only stopped when word of its savagery filtered south and sickened the nation.

Many lairds were to have been excluded from the Act of Indemnity of 1747, but a list of those to have their estates confiscated which included the lairds of Blairfettie and Faskally was never put into effect and the lands of Struan, which were forfeited in 1689 and never properly restored to the old chief, was the only Clan Donnachaidh property annexed by the government.

Virtually the only recorded resistance in Atholl after Culloden came from old Rob Ban of Invervack who lost two sons in the battle. In the autumn of 1746 he tricked nine redcoats resting by the roadside north of Tummel Bridge into surrendering their weapons to him. He was recognised when he later went to Inverness and was thrown into prison, but was released on the intervention of Robertson of Inches. This family, descended from Duncan the third chief, had long been landowners and successful merchants in the north. Rob Ban is said to have lived to be 101.

Another old recalcitrant was Duncan of Auchleeks. He refused to obey the laws against Highland dress and wore tartan and carried a dirk till his dying day. He also drank to the 'King over the Water', as they called the exiled Stuart claimant to the throne, each evening but his son joined the army and he must drink the health of King George. The toast

'The King' safely covered both consciences. The loyal toast remained a problem for some. Finger bowls were not permitted at dinners in Buckingham Palace until the reign of Edward VII at the beginning of the 20th century. This was to prevent closet Jacobites passing their glasses across the bowl, and hence the water, during the loyal toast.

Chapter Twelve

The Destruction of the Clan System

B y 1745, the United Kingdom was well on his way to creating the foundations of a modern state but the Highlands existed in a time warp, its culture utterly different from the rest of the country. Even thirty years later in 1775, Dr Samuel Johnson could still write 'To the Southern inhabitants of Scotland, the state of the mountains and the islands is equally unknown with that of Borneo or Sumatra; of both they have heard little and guess the rest.' and this gives some idea of how Lowlanders and the London government must have viewed the Highlands.

The differences were intolerable and the redcoat rampage was deliberately designed to destroy the culture that could send up to 30,000 trained warriors pouring down into the peaceful south. This was backed by law. Weapons were confiscated; the hereditary legal powers of the chiefs - which included the Duke of Atholl and all the little Robertson baronies which gave the lairds authority over their tenants - were removed; the wearing of the kilt and tartan made illegal; the Gaelic language suppressed; bagpipes declared to be instruments of war and Robert Reid was hanged after a trial in Carlisle for playing them. Thousands of supposed rebels were executed, transported or died in prison hulks.

Had Prince Charles never come to Scotland the clan society of the Highlands would have quietly decayed under the impact of the Industrial Revolution. In fact this process was already well under way by 1745. But the Rising, and the savage effectiveness of the government in exterminating the way of life that spawned its soldiers and could spawn them again, gave the death of this society a focus and a tragic romance that echoes down the centuries.

In this new world, landowners needed cash, not armed followers, and sheep produced more money than tenants. Superfluous young men joined the Highland Regiments. Forming these was a stroke of genius by the government. The bagpipes, the kilt, tartan, the broadsword and all weapons were banned - except in the service of his Majesty.

Highlander in the British Army.

In the Highland regiments and only in the Highland regiments could the young Gael enjoy, like his honoured forefathers, the warrior culture and all its trappings. At least fifty thousand young Highlanders, who would in other times have been warriors in the tails of their chiefs and lairds, were siphoned off to fight for the Crown. The Black Watch, the 42nd Regiment, was the first choice of the young men of Atholl. It was the first of the Highland Regiments, embodied at Wade's Taybridge in 1739 and had its origins in the old Independent Companies set up to police the Highlands after the earlier Rising of 1715.

Clansmen had already made their mark as soldiers in the Scots contingents of an assortment of European armies before 1745 and been sending back money to their families in Atholl for generations. At Fontenoy in 1745 the British advance had been halted by the Scots Regiment in the French service and this gave the French their victory. The night before the battle, their officers came across to the British camp and been entertained by the Black Watch for many were each other's kinsmen and friends. And many on both sides would become the core of the Prince's rebel army. Later in the century, Clansmen fought against the French and her allies in North America, in the Caribbean, in India, Europe, Africa, South America and against the rebellious colonies in America and the United States in 1812. In America particularly, many chose to stay when their service was completed and joined other Highlanders who had emigrated in their thousands since the early 18th century.

Stemming from the family of Lude, whom themselves used the surnames Duncanson and Reid in early years, are the Reid-Robertsons of Straloch, just across the watershed east of Pitlochry. They dominated Strathardle and their kindred at one time or another held eighteen estates. The head of the family was known as the Baron Reid and the last of the main line, John Reid, was an accomplished flute player who joined the Black Watch in 1745 and was taken prisoner by the rebels at Prestonpans. He was freed and was later responsible for the capture of treasure from France to finance the rebel campaign which was landed from the sloop Prince Charles in northern Scotland in March 1746. Its loss ensured the end of the Rising after Culloden. He fought in the Americas and went on to become a general, a composer and left his fortune to found a chair of Music at Edinburgh University. A concert is held in the city each year in his memory; the opening piece is one of Reid's own works 'The Garb of Old Gaul'.

General Reid of Straloch.

Struan's heir was a descendant of his great uncle Duncan Mor of Drumachuine who was younger brother and stout right arm to the Tutor of Struan, leader of the Athollmen in Montrose's wars. The new chief, Duncan, had known he was likely successor for some time and he knew his predecessor's legal hold on the family lands was rather fragile. He needed a firmer legal foundation to ensure his succession and he was just about to obtain his own charter on the chief's lands when Prince Charles landed in 1745.

Duncan said later he 'laboured under a dangerous illness' at the start of the Rising but it did not stop him doing all he could to help. Certainly enough to ensure that he was high on the wanted list when the rebellion collapsed. He was one of eighty people named in the Act of Indemnity of 1747 as excluded from the general pardon to those who had been engaged in the Rising. Rather than fleeing abroad he was advised to stay in Scotland to be on hand when old Alexander died to ensure his inheritance. So he 'skulked', the term used for those sought by the redcoats who flitted through the Highlands or sheltered with friends with an escape route always ready to take them back to the hills and forests.

From Culloden till July 1753 Duncan skulked, mostly in Atholl. He recorded that he stayed in 157 different places, from Lord Forbes' castle in Aberdeenshire to Donald Ban's barn on Loch Rannoch. On the old chief's death, he 'ordered my wife and children to repair to Carie, and possess a little Hutt that was built after the burning in 1746.' The tenants paid their rents to the new chief's trustees but the authorities refused to countenance this and eventually threatened his entire family with military execution unless they left the area. Eventually Duncan took his wife and their four small children - and the Clach na Bratach, always the personal property of the chief - to Edinburgh. They caught a ship from Leith and arrived, virtually destitute, in Paris where they joined other exiled rebels. A friend wrote to Blairfettie, by then a captain in Ogilvy's Regiment of the Scots Brigade. 'Mr Robertson of Drumocharn (who ought now to be Strowan) is come to Dunkirk with his wife and family. God knows what will become of them. I'm afraid it will be difficult to get him a gratification and he dare not return home'. James, still a king in exile, sent him 1,000 livres.

The '45 marked the end of clan culture but it seems that the change in Atholl had come earlier. With its territory on the edge of the

Highlands, the Clan Donnachaidh had always been more exposed to economic and cultural influences from the south than clans in more remote parts of the country. Nobody can look at the Highlands today without marvelling that so hard a country and difficult a climate could support the population that it did, but if there were opportunities for greater prosperity only a fool would ignore them.

As Herbert Robertson wrote in 1893 'The last final migration of the agricultural population took place during the American War, when certain manufactures were started in the villages at the entrance to the Highlands, Blairgowrie, Dunkeld, etc. and the Robertson Clan being the nearest to these villages flocked into them. The manufactures have long ceased to exist, but the Robertsons were obliged to remain in the Lowland villages and they still form a considerable portion of the population. The Robertsons now found in great numbers in the large towns of Scotland - Glasgow, Edinburgh, and Aberdeen, especially the latter - and throughout England and the British Empire, but these last can almost all trace back to the time, rarely more than a century ago, when their ancestors lived in Scotland. In all families, whether living in Scotland or elsewhere, the tradition of a Perthshire origin is universal.'

Struan's lands were put under the management of the Commissioners for the Forfeited Estates. Ensign James Small was the long-time factor who set up house at Carie. In the rentals of 1755, he provides a snapshot of the population.

There were 1235 inhabitants in families averaging five in size. Half were under the age of seventeen. Only a fifth could speak English. Just under half the families were named Robertson, the next most common names were Cameron and Campbell. Conspicuous by their absence were any Macgregors. Since the name had been proscribed by James VI, they masqueraded under aliases - Dow, Anderson, Murray amongst others.

111 families lived on the south side of Loch Rannoch and further west. Kinloch Rannoch and the Mount Alexander farms held 53 families. Fearnan on Loch Tay 62, and the lands still owned by the chief in Glen Errochty and Invervack 52.

If one looks at the Faskally Court Record for 1743 which covers the area from, roughly, Struan Kirk down to Pitlochry, one finds that about a third of the names mentioned are Robertsons. The next most common name is Stewart with under 9%. These proportions seem to be typical at this time. As was stated in 1895, Clansfolk had been leaving Atholl for years, to the Lowlands, as mercenaries for hire to Continental armies, to Ireland and to the Americas.

The old poet had been much loved by his people but he had left his estates to moulder. The Commissioners and Ensign Small began improvements, often biting off more than they could chew. Before the '45, Rannoch was one of the most remote, poverty-stricken, and backward regions of the Highlands but this changed. Amid the government's policy of cultural genocide applied after the '45, the record of the Commissioners for the Forfeited Estates is a light in the darkness of persecution. Matters such as agricultural improvements, the creation of infrastructure, industry, and raising the living standards of the people were not on Struan's list. These were the priorities of the factors on the confiscated estates.

Redcoats surveying for roads in Rannoch.

The village of Kinloch Rannoch was created in the period after the '45. Redcoats built roads from Tummel Bridge and round the side of

Schiehallion. The river was bridged adjacent to the new settlement. Initially this was to be populated by retired soldiers who would act as long term insurance against further rebellions, but they could not cope with the bucolic rhythms of a croft and so Rannoch people were given leases for their own few acres for the first time.

The factors encouraged the linen industry by building little water-powered weaving mills. Craftsmen moved in to keep the machinery in repair. This brought cash into the community and gave more economic power to the women who did all the spinning. Timber from the Black Wood was exploited. Lime burning was introduced to reduce the natural acidity of the soil and grow more crops, particularly the potato.

At one time the Commissioners intended to drive a road across Rannoch moor to Glencoe and thus make Kinloch Rannoch the hub of the Highlands. 250 years later, the road is still occasionally mooted. The redcoats built themselves a barracks at the head of the loch and continued their road westwards for a few miles before it vanished into the bogs. They were even put to work in a futile attempt to drain parts of the moor and make it cultivable. Today the scars are still visible.

Chapter Thirteen
The Tartan Revival

'His wisdom, family orientation, sage advice and kindliness all mark him out as an exceptional gentleman.' Thus wrote a descendant of Duncan Robertson of Struan. He died in exile at Givet in France in 1782. His daughter married Laurence Oliphant of Gask and their daughter was Carolina Nairne whose hauntingly romantic songs such as 'Will ye no'come back again?', 'The Rowan Tree', 'The Auld Hoose', 'Wi' a hundred pipers' are still popular today.

Alexander, the 15th chief.

The estates were restored to Duncan's son in 1784. Colonel Alexander Robertson, 15th chief, was born in 1740. He and his brother Walter were educated in France and Holland and became officers in the Scots Brigade in the service of the Dutch States-General. He returned to Atholl when the war against the American colonies broke out and raised a battalion for service in the British Army. He was described by David Stewart of Garth: 'The race of Bradwardine is not long extinct. In my own time several veterans might have set for the picture, so admirably drawn in Waverley [by Sir Walter Scott] of that most honourable, brave, learned, and kind-hearted personage, the Baron of Bradwardine. These gentlemen returned from the Continent, full of warlike Latin, French phrases, and inveterate broad Scots (learned, as I have said, by the Highlanders abroad). One, I believe of the last of these, was Colonel Alexander Robertson of the Scots Brigade.'

Mount Alexander, built 1796.

Alexander, a bachelor, lived at Rannoch Barracks at the west end of the loch. Stewart of Garth in 1815 wrote that 'except when at funerals and on days of mourning, he always wears Highland Dress, and a fine figure he makes in it, for I know not a more elegant looking man, nor more the looks of a gentleman.' He built a new house at Dunalastair. His heir was his third cousin, Capt Alexander Robertson, descendant of Rob Ban of Invervack. He was born in France in 1745 and served in the British Army during the American War in which he was severely wounded. He succeeded Colonel Alexander in 1822, and died in 1830. A description of him operating the Clach-na-Bratach survives. 'Mr. Robertson well remembered seeing the old soldier - a man remarkable for the stately courtesy of his manners - with much ceremonious gravity dip this crystal in a great china bowl filled with spring water (a fairy spring it was, the name of which I have unfortunately forgot), which he then distributed to a number of people who had come great distances to obtain it for medical purposes.' The water most probably came from the Fairy Well on the east flank of Schiehallion to which the locals had resorted for Beltane celebrations for centuries.

General George Duncan Robertson, 17th Chief.

The chief's estates were heavily mortgaged. His remaining land in Glen Errochty and Invervack was sold to the Duke of Atholl in 1826. In

George Duncan Robertson,
18th Chief.

a typically dubious deal the Earl of Breadalbane had bought Fearnan by Loch Tay from the Forfeited Estates Commissioners, so the chief's lands were restricted to Rannoch. Another cousin, General George Duncan Robertson, became Struan in 1830 and his namesake and son who succeeded was the last chief with a significant estate in Clan country. He sold the house at Dunalastair to another local laird, General John Macdonald of Dalchosnie, married to the daughter of McInroy of Lude, in 1853 who promptly demolished it and built the mansion now in ruins there today. All that was reserved for the family was the burial ground.

The 18th chief built Dall House in the Black Wood in 1855 but was forced to sell it a few years later.

Dall House on Loch Rannoch.

Alastair Stewart Robertson,
the 20th Chief.

The Robertsons of Struan were left with the Barracks which was built for redcoats after the '45 at the west end of Loch Rannoch and 19,000 acres. This may sound large, but land on Rannoch Moor is good for bogs, rocks and moss but little else. Even this was sold in 1926. The chief's heir was his uncle, Alastair Gilbert, one of two brothers who, like many others, had emigrated to the West Indies to grow sugar. He died in 1884 without having returned to Scotland.

His son Alastair Stewart became the 20th Chief. A bachelor, he was enthusiastic about the Clan's heritage and largely responsible for reforming the Clan Society in 1893. He died in 1910. His successor, George Duncan, was a distinguished public servant and Mayor of Kingston in Jamaica. His eldest son Langton, a historian and schoolmaster, became 22nd chief in 1949 and enjoyed an emotional return to Scotland and Clan Country in 1970. Langton's

George Duncan, 21st Chief.

son Gilbert who farms in Kent became 23rd chief of the Clan Donnachaidh in 1983.

Lude was the oldest cadet family of Struan whose lands ran with those of the Duke of Atholl to the east of Blair Castle. In 1803 it was inherited by General William Robertson who feuded with his neighbour. The general encouraged his tenants to trespass and even fired cannon onto the Duke's ground to scare away the deer. The two parties went to law and the general lost.

Langton, 22nd Chief.

When a colonel, he had been the first commanding officer of the Perthshire regiment of Fencibles 1797-99 which was one of many such home defence formations designed to counter the threat of invasion by Napoleon. In 1808 he founded the Loyal Clan Donachy Volunteers. Command was held by his son, a major who had served in the Atholl Highlanders, one of the fifty regiments raised in the Highlands to fight thee French. The Volunteers had three companies, the 1st was recruited on Lude and the second in Glen Errochty. The third company was the mounted artillery. The general was obviously an awkward character and his regiment did not survive his reluctance to amalgamate with other volunteer forces. Soon after his death, debts forced the sale of his ancient estate. The last Robertson laird drowned himself in the river Tilt in 1820.

The road engineer, Joseph Mitchell, writing of the years in the first quarter of the 19th century, painted a rosy picture - clearly he never visited Lude - but one which was soon to change as the economy collapsed. 'The Highlands of Perthshire presented at this time, a picture of great rural happiness...almost all the lairds lived on their properties, engaged in improvements, took an interest in their tenants, and promoted by their influence the advancement of clever lads who were born on their estates...To me, an outsider, looking back, this district at that time exhibited a very happy state of society. Each class was contented in its own sphere, and, as far as I could tell, there were few jealousies. The whole people were comfortable, and lived and moved among each other in a genial and kindly atmosphere'

Towards the end of the eighteenth century the Highlands began to be fashionable. James Macpherson produced a volume of poems purporting to be by the ancient Gaelic writer Ossian and these took Europe by storm, even becoming Napoleon's preferred campaign reading. Rousseau introduced the concept of the Noble Savage which fitted the Highlander admirably. Dr Johnson met Flora MacDonald who had helped Prince Charles to escape and published his account of the meeting and his tour of the Highlands in 1775. And the courage of the Highland regiments in the British army attracted the admiration of the world.

The penal legislation introduced after the '45 was lifted in 1782, thanks to pressure from the gentry, particularly the Highland Society of London. They sponsored piping contests and Highland games to encourage manly pursuits amongst the people. It was these lairds who set out the framework of what we now consider the traditional culture of Gaeldom. An example of their inventiveness can be found in tartan. In the old days, the Highlander used the colours she could find in the plants of her neighbourhood to tint the wool and there is some evidence to suggest that the prevalence of certain dyestuffs in a district gave raise to a similarity in local tartans. This was taken a stage further. In consultation with the chiefs the Highland Society came up with the idea that each clan had its own tartan.

Andrew Robertson, a miniature portrait painter, first suggested a register of clan tartans. David Stewart of Garth took it upon himself to write round the chiefs. He asked his friend Col. Alexander Robertson of Struan to send in a sample of the Clan's tartan. The answer came back 'More than twenty years ago I wished to ascertain what the pattern of the Clandonachy Tartan was, and applied to different old men of the Clan for information, most of whom pretended to know what the pattern was, but as no two of the descriptions I received were exactly similar, and as they were all very vulgar and gaudy, I did not think proper to adopt any of them'. He went on to say that he wore the Atholl tartan, of which Stewart said there were two patterns, since his forebears had once owned the whole district.

One suspects Struan had hit the nail on the head. Tartans were gaudy - that was their point - the gaudier the better because a good loud red had once required rare and expensive dyes and signalled wealth. But, although some case could be made for local area tartans, of clan links there was little trace. Stewart told Andrew Robertson about it. 'A few more years as you justly observe and the memory of such things will be lost, and the truth of this cannot be a stronger proof than that Strowan does not properly know what his own Tartan is.' It does not cross his mind that the memory may not have been so much lost as never having been there at all. Alexander did eventually produce a sample of tartan authenticated with his seal and signature but this, the first Clan Donnachaidh tartan, bears no relation to the Clan patterns today.

In 1822, George IV visited Edinburgh, the first monarch to come to Scotland since Charles II. Sir Walter Scott helped by Garth, laid on a tartan extravaganza in Edinburgh. Highland chiefs gathered their tenants and came to parade in front of the king and the people of Edinburgh. Struan was an old man, a few months from death, and so Clan Donnachaidh did not send a contingent. The Lowland spectators were dazzled and decided to claim this romantic version of Gaeldom as their own heritage, an appropriation further cultivated by the Victorians. It had little to do with reality but served as a powerful focus for national pride which assisted the Scottish identity to survive the overwhelming proximity of its larger neighbour.

But agricultural prices had crashed at the end of the Napoleonic wars. Many of the old lairds with their old paternal attitudes were swept away by their debts and their tenants faced new landlords who needed to rationalise their estates if they were not to go the way of their predecessors. To stay afloat, many chiefs and other land owners forced people off their farms and off their estates in the infamous clearances. In 1823, the Duke of Atholl was described by Stewart of Garth as a 'grinding and cruel oppressor' for his treatment of his tenants, but no clearances took place on Clan estates in Atholl. Perhaps that is one reason why none of the old chieftains' estates are still owned by their descendants.

David Stewart of Garth.

Of course Clansfolk remained in the straths, but the culture was no longer theirs. The extravaganza of George IV's visit could only work because the society it glorified and caricatured no longer constituted a threat. It had already gone. Scholars were collecting the fragments that remained and writing books to explain the customs of the mountains to a growing audience. The huge success of the romantic movement and Walter Scott's Highland novels and romances brought tourists north to see the landscape that he wrote about. And the interest of the royal family which began with George IV and his brothers was intensified by Queen Victoria and Prince Albert who visited both Blair and Taymouth castles to enjoy bagpipes, deer stalking and dancing Highlanders before buying themselves Balmoral.

Struan Kirk.

Clan spirit never disappeared in Atholl. The old Highland society depended upon kinship to cement it together. People knew they were related to their chief and could shake his hand when they met him and this created a bond very different from the conventional one between landlord and tenant. Ask in Gaelic from where a man comes and the question literally translates as from whom does he come. Genealogy was the corner stone of the culture, fitting each person into the community and linking him or her to everyone else. This became irrelevant in the Lowlands or overseas because those societies had different values and so the ability of everyone to reel off generations of their forebears was lost. Perhaps someone took the trouble to note down or remember some of the anecdotage of an ancient relative, but the pin-sharp precision had gone and today it is difficult for many Clansfolk to discover their particular niche in the network of kinship that stemmed from Atholl.

Those who remained were very conscious of their history and efforts to preserve it and Clan spirit are in evidence even before the death of the last survivors of Culloden. An event which galvanised the Clan in 1821 was the attempt by the Duke of Atholl to close Struan Kirk. A fellow clansman wrote to Duncan Robertson of Kindrochit on the subject. 'You have heard something of the ungracious attempt made by the Dictator of Atholl to do away with the Auld Kirk of Strowan. I presume you know His Grace is now become proprietor of that pendicle on which the Church of Strowan stands, and it would appear he wishes to exert his Overwhelming Authority to make a clean sweep of everything that was formerly held sacred by the Clan of Robertson.' His Grace was thwarted and a new church built.

Chapter Fourteen
The Clan Society

The Clan Donnachaidh Society was inaugurated at a dinner in Edinburgh in 1823. Struan was in the chair and his deputy was Capt Duncan Robertson of Kindrochit who substituted for General Robertson, Struan's heir. The chief's piper piped and Nathaniel Gow, son of the great Niel and almost as distinguished a musician, provided the band. Nine months earlier Gow had entertained the king at Dalkeith House.

In June that year, Struan called a meeting of 'Clan Robertson in Athole' at which he suggested 'that it would be a most desirable event to form an association with the Clan Stewart within the bounds of Athole, as in ancient times, for the purpose of promoting and cementing a generous, manly, and Brotherly friendship between the two Clans, such as subsisted between their ancestors, also to revive and cherish a proper Highland spirit and feeling among the members of the two Clans, and give encouragement to every species of industry, for which this part of the Country is well adapted, and especially the manufacture at home and the general adoption of dress of those fabricks which have ever been peculiar to the Highlands, namely Tartans, Plaids, and Bonnets.'

The meeting ran with the idea and formed the Association of Atholemen the following November. This eventually evolved into 'The Gathering of the Men of Athole' which still meets in the grounds of Blair Castle each year. The original committee shows that both Stewarts and Robertsons were still substantial landholders:

Captain Robertson of Strowan

Col Stewart of Garth

Mr McInroy or Robertson of Lude

Mr Stewart of Foss

Mr Robertson of Auchleeks

Dr Stewart of Bonskeid

Capt Robertson of Edradynate

Mr Stewart of Derculich

Mr Alex Robertson Auchanree

Capt Stewart of Shierglass

Capt G. Stewart Allain

Capt Robertson of Kindrochit

Of the Clan Donnachaidh names, James McInroy, descended from the Reid-Robertsons of Straloch, was son of an Atholl farmer. He made a fortune based on West Indies sugar and bought Lude under the nose of the Duke of Atholl. The MacInroys also bought Shierglass, the estate on the opposite hillside across the river Garry, and held it until 1939. Auchleeks was sold out of the Clan in 1962, Edradynate in 1969, Kindrochit in 1883, Blairfettie in 1821. Auchanree in Glen Errochty and Allain on Loch Tummel were owned by the Duke of Atholl by 1826.

Duncan Robertson of Kindrochit.
The first Clan Society Secretary.

There was another Clan Donnachaidh lunch in Edinburgh in 1824. By the following year this had developed into the Clan Donnachaidh Society with activities also taking place in Glasgow and at least one overseas member in the shape of Dr William Robertson in Montreal. The last formal dinner of this earliest incarnation of the Society seems to have been held in 1842. The outstanding funds were turned into a trust and used to pay the schoolmaster of Struan and today the trustees, direct descendants of the cadet families of Kindrochit and Invervack who were instrumental in founding the Society, still support the school at Struan and others in Highland Perthshire.

The Society continued in a desultory fashion and was re-formed in 1893 with district secretaries in Canada and Australia as well as throughout the UK. Life members came from across the British Empire as well as New York, Chicago, North Carolina and New Jersey. With the enthusiastic support of the 20th Chief the Society met annually and flourished until 1914 and the catastrophe of the Great War. It continued in a truncated form between the wars with Clan dinners being held in various Scottish towns but it sprang to vigorous life again in 1948.

Clan Centre.

The first Clan Annual was published in 1951 and it has come out regularly ever since and, for half a century, the magazine has been privileged to have some of Scotland's leading historians contributing to it.

In 1969, the Clan Society - which now has some 25 branches across the world - created the first purpose-built Clan Museum in Scotland at Bruar in the heart of Clan country. Here is displayed the Clach na Bratach, weapons used at Culloden and other treasures of the Clan as well as an archive, library, interactive computers and up-to-date interpretations of the Clan and its history. It provides a focus for the descendants of those whose forbears lived in these hills and glens and often fought and sometimes died to defend them. But its main objective is to cherish the story of one great Highland family, the Clan Donnachaidh, for the benefit of the nation and the many thousands of people from across the world whose origins are to be found in Clan country.

The Museum in 1970.

Sir Edward Reid, Bridgit Robertson, King Robert Bruce, Catriona Robertson, Gilbert Robertson of Drumachuine and Langton, 22nd Chief.

Appendices

Septs: A sept is usually defined as people of a different name from that carried by most Clansfolk who lived in the country of the Clan and were fully integrated, fighting with it, and usually linked by blood. Before Robert Riabhach, the common designation of the chief's family was de Atholia, although Robert and his brothers were named as Duncansons in the 1392 Act of Forfeiture. After him they used Robertson and many cadets - offshoots of the chief's line - followed them. Most Clansmen still neither needed nor used a surname although Clandonquhy, or something similar, could fulfil this function as in John Dow Mc Enos Vc Condoquhy who died in 1564. When surnames were generally adopted in the 18th century, a myriad of different names were utilised, many referring to some immediate forebear, or some derivation from Duncan, or from a nickname. In the Duke of Atholl's Fencible Men 1705-6, for example, are such oddities as Sool, Gadaiche, McAlastair mohoir, McCamachasich, Coinic, McCononchies Ban and Dubh, Robertson alias Clarsair, alias Gilbert, alias McGregor, alias Fraoch, Douglas (Reid), McMhaolagain, McAlestair Buie. All these likely evolved into modern surnames associated with the Clan.

Reid was early used by branches of the Clan distinguished by red hair. The leading cadet family of this name called themselves Reid-Robertsons until the 18th century when they dropped his second barrel. The accepted list of sept names used by the Clan and its kindred are Collier, Colyear - used by the earls of Portmore, Connachie, Conochie, Cunnison, Dobbie, Dobbin, Dobie, Dobieson, Dobinson, Dobson, Donachie, Donachy, Duncanson, Dunnachie, Hobson Inches, Kynoch, MacConachie, MacConchie, MacConechy, MacConich, MacConnochie, MacDonachie, MacGlashan, MacInroy, MacIver, MacIvor, MacJames, MacLagan, MacCullich, MacOnachie, MacRobbie, MacRobert, MacRoberts, MacRobie, MacWilliam, Read, Reed, Robbie, Roberts, Robinson, Robson, Roy, Skene, Stark, Tonnochy. Spelling did not become standardised until well into the 19th century so many variations exist on these names but they all stem from the Clan.

Pipe Music: **STRUAN ROBERTSON'S SALUTE.**

The Robertsons have Come
Turn the Cattle, Donnachie
The Blue Ribbon
The Coming of the Robertsons
Lament for Robertson of Struan

Clan Badges: The existence of plant badges likely confirms that Clan tartans are comparatively modern. To show that they were part of the Clan Donnachaidh, warriors wore either fine-leaved heath (*erica cinerea*) or fern (*felix*) in their bonnets.

Arms: The Clan badge is shown on the front cover and this can be worn by all members of the Clan. Individual clansmen can apply to Lord Lyon for their own coats-of-arms which usually show a variation on those of the Chief. His arms are described as: Gules, three wolves' heads erased argent, armed and langued azure. Crest: A dexter arm couped in pale holding a regal crown proper, and under the escutcheon a wild man chained proper. Supporters: On the dexter side, A serpent; and on the sinister, A dove, the head of each encircled in rays. Motto: *Virtutis gloria merces* (Glory is the reward of virtue.)

Struan's Arms.

From this description, the blazoner could draw the arms as he pleased.

Two variations are shown. The first from about 1820 and the second a modern interpretation. The latter also shows the Clan slogan or war cry: *'Garg'n Uair Dhuisgear'* - Fierce when Roused.

Chief List:

I   Duncan 1275-1355
II   Robert de Atholia
III   Duncan (Crosda) de Atholia
IV   Robert (Riabhach) de Atholia d.1461
V   Alexander Robertson d.1505
         succeeded by his grandson
VI   William Robertson of Strowan executed
VII   Robert Robertson of Strowan d.1566
VIII   William Robertson of Strowan d.1588
         succeeded by his brother
IX   Donald Robertson of Strowan
X   Robert Robertson of Strowan d.c1630
XI   Alexander Robertson of Strowan d.1636
XII   Alexander Robertson of Strowan d.1688
XIII   Alexander Robertson of Strowan d.1749
         succeeded by a cousin
XIV   Duncan Robertson of Strowan d.1782
XV   Alexander Robertson of Strowan d.1822
         succeeded by a cousin
XVI   Alexander Robertson of Strowan d.1830
XVII   George Duncan Robertson of Strowan d.1842
XVIII   George Duncan Robertson of Strowan d.1864
         succeeded by his uncle
XIX   Alexander Gilbert Robertson of Strowan
XX   Alasdair Stewart Robertson d.1910
         succeeded by a cousin.
XXI   George Duncan Robertson of Struan d.1949
XXII   Langton George Duncan Haldane of Struan d.1983
XXIII   Alexander Gilbert Haldane Robertson of Struan

For enquiries about membership of the Clan Society,
for details of the Clan DNA Program, or anything
else, contact:

The Clan Donnachaidh Society

Clan Donnachaidh Centre,
Bruar,
Pitlochry,
Perthshire
PH18 5TW

+44 (0)1796 483 338

clandonnachaidh@compuserve.com

www.donnachaidh.com